MATH TRAILBLAZERS™

Grade 4

Facts Resource Guide

×	0	1	2	3	4	5	6	7	8	9	10
0	0	0	0	0	0	0	0	0	0	0	0
1	0	1	2	3	4	5	6	7	8	9	10
2	0	2	4	6	8	10	12	14	16	18	20
3	0	3	6	9	12	15	18	21	24	27	30
4	0	4	8	12	16	20	24	28	32	36	40
5	0	5	10	15	20	25	30	35	40	45	50
6	0	6	12	18	24	30	36	42	48	54	60
7	0	7	14	21	28	35	42	49	56	63	70
8	0	8	16	24	32	40	48	56	64	72	80
9	0	9	18	27	36	45	54	63	72	81	90
10	0	10	20	30	40	50	60	70	80	90	100

Second Edition

A Mathematical Journey Using Science and Language Arts

T 79316

KENDALL/HUNT PUBLISHING COMPANY
4050 Westmark Drive   Dubuque, Iowa 52002

A TIMS® Curriculum
University of Illinois at Chicago

UIC The University of Illinois
at Chicago

The original edition was based on work supported by the National Science Foundation under grant No. MDR 9050226 and the University of Illinois at Chicago. Any opinions, findings, and conclusions or recommendations expressed in this publication are those of the author(s) and do not necessarily reflect the views of the granting agencies.

Grade 4 · Acknowledgments

TIMS Elementary Mathematics Curriculum Project

Teaching Integrated Mathematics and Science (TIMS) Project Directors
Philip Wagreich, Principal Investigator
Joan L. Bieler
Marty Gartzman
Howard Goldberg (emeritus)
Catherine Randall Kelso

Director, Second Edition
Catherine Randall Kelso

Curriculum Developers, Second Edition
Lindy M. Chambers-Boucher
Elizabeth Colligan
Marty Gartzman
Carol Inzerillo
Catherine Randall Kelso
Jennifer Mundt Leimberer
Georganne E. Marsh
Leona Peters
Philip Wagreich

Editorial and Production Staff, Second Edition
Kathleen R. Anderson
Ai-Ai C. Cojuangco
Andrada Costoiu
Erika Larson
Georganne E. Marsh
Cosmina Menghes
Anne Roby
Kathy Vondracek

TIMS Professional Developers
Barbara Crum
Craig Cleve
Elizabeth Colligan
Pamela Guyton
Carol Inzerillo
Linda Miceli
Leona Peters
Jane Schlichting

TIMS Director of Media Services
Henrique Cirne-Lima

TIMS Research Staff
Catherine Randall Kelso
Barry Booton
Dibyen Majumdar

TIMS Administrative Staff
Ora Benton
David Cirillo
Enrique Puente

Principal Investigators, First Edition
Philip Wagreich, Project Director
Howard Goldberg

Senior Curriculum Developers, First Edition

Joan L. Bieler
Janet Simpson Beissinger
Astrida Cirulis
Marty Gartzman
Howard Goldberg

Carol Inzerillo
Andy Isaacs
Catherine Randall Kelso
Leona Peters
Philip Wagreich

Curriculum Developers, First Edition

Janice C. Banasiak
Lynne Beauprez
Andy Carter
Lindy M. Chambers-Boucher
Kathryn Chval
Diane Czerwinski

Jenny Knight
Sandy Niemiera
Janice Ozima
Polly Tangora
Paul Trafton

Illustrator, First Edition
Kris Dresen

Research Consultant, First Edition
Andy Isaacs

Mathematics Education Consultant, First Edition
Paul Trafton

National Advisory Committee, First Edition

Carl Berger
Tom Berger
Hugh Burkhardt
Donald Chambers
Naomi Fisher
Glenda Lappan

Mary Lindquist
Eugene Maier
Lourdes Monteagudo
Elizabeth Phillips
Thomas Post

Grade

Table of Contents

Background

Math Trailblazers™ includes a comprehensive, research-based program for teaching basic math facts. This program is carefully integrated into the lessons and Daily Practice and Problems (DPP) of each grade and the Home Practice in Grades 3–5. The *Grade 4 Facts Resource Guide* is a compilation of much of the math facts materials for fourth grade. These include math facts lessons, relevant DPP items, Home Practice parts, flash cards, *Facts I Know* charts, the TIMS Tutor: *Math Facts,* and information for parents about the *Math Trailblazers* math facts philosophy.

Classrooms that stay close to the suggested pacing schedule for teaching lessons will have little difficulty implementing the complete math facts program without the use of this guide. In those classrooms, teachers can simply use the math facts materials that are built into the lessons, Daily Practice and Problems, and Home Practice. However, because the math facts program is closely linked to the recommended schedule for teaching lessons, classrooms that differ significantly from the suggested pacing of units will need to make special accommodations in order to ensure that students receive a consistent program of math facts practice and assessment throughout the year. This manual will assist teachers with that process. (A pacing schedule can be found in the Grade 4 Overview section in the *Teacher Implementation Guide*.)

All of the materials included in the *Grade 4 Facts Resource Guide* are located elsewhere in *Math Trailblazers.* Wherever appropriate, we will include a reference to an item's location in other *Math Trailblazers* components.

A major goal of *Math Trailblazers* is to prepare students to compute accurately, flexibly, and appropriately in all situations. Standard topics in arithmetic—acquisition of basic math facts and fluency with whole-number operations—are covered extensively.

In developing our program for the math facts, we sought a careful balance between strategies and drill. This approach is based on a large body of research and advocated by the National Council of Teachers of Mathematics (NCTM) *Principles and Standards for School Mathematics* and by the National Research Council in *Adding It Up: Helping Children Learn Mathematics*. The research indicates that the methods used in the *Math Trailblazers* math facts program lead to more effective learning and better retention of the math facts and also help develop essential math skills.

For a detailed discussion of the math facts program in *Math Trailblazers,* see Section 3 TIMS Tutor: *Math Facts*. See also Section 2 *Information for Parents: Math Facts Philosophy.*

What Is the Math Trailblazers Facts Resource Guide?

Introduction to the Math Facts in *Math Trailblazers*

The following table describes the development of math facts and whole-number operations in *Math Trailblazers*. The shaded portions of the table highlight development of the math facts program in each grade. Expectations for fluency with math facts are indicated in bold. The white portions of the table highlight development of the whole-number operations.

Grade	Addition	Subtraction	Multiplication	Division
K	Introduce concepts through problem solving and use of manipulatives.			
1	Develop strategies for addition facts.	Develop strategies for subtraction facts.	Develop concepts through problem solving and use of manipulatives.	
	Solve addition problems in context.	Solve subtraction problems in context.		
2	Continue use of addition facts in problems. Continue use of strategies for addition facts. **Assess for fluency with addition facts.**	Continue use of subtraction facts in problems. Continue use of strategies for subtraction facts. **Assess for fluency with subtraction facts.**	Continue concept development through problem solving and use of manipulatives.	
	Continue solving addition problems in context. Introduce procedures for multidigit addition using manipulatives and paper and pencil.	Continue solving subtraction problems in context. Introduce procedures for multidigit subtraction using manipulatives and paper and pencil.		
3	Diagnose and remediate with addition facts as needed.	Maintain fluency with subtraction facts through review and assessment.	Continue use of multiplication facts in problems. Develop strategies for multiplication facts. **Assess for fluency with multiplication facts.**	Continue use of division facts in problems. Develop strategies for division facts.
	Develop procedures for multi-digit addition using manipulatives and paper and pencil. Practice and apply multidigit addition in varied contexts.	Develop procedures for multidigit subtraction using manipulatives and paper and pencil. Practice and apply multidigit subtraction in varied contexts.	Solve multiplication problems in context. Introduce paper-and-pencil multiplication (1-digit $\times$ 2-digits).	Continue concept development. Solve division problems in context.
4	Diagnose and remediate with addition facts as needed.	Diagnose and remediate with subtraction facts as needed.	Maintain fluency with multiplication facts through review and assessment.	Continue use of division facts in problems. Continue development of strategies for division facts. **Assess for fluency with division facts.**
	Practice and apply multidigit addition in varied contexts. Review paper-and-pencil procedures for multidigit addition.	Practice and apply multidigit subtraction in varied contexts. Review paper-and-pencil procedures for multidigit subtraction.	Develop procedures for multi-plication using manipulatives and paper and pencil (1-digit and 2-digit multipliers). Practice and apply multipli-cation in varied contexts.	Solve division problems in context. Develop procedures for division using manipulatives and paper and pencil (1-digit divisors).
5	Diagnose and remediate with addition facts as needed.	Diagnose and remediate with subtraction facts as needed.	Maintain fluency with multiplication facts through review and assessment.	Maintain fluency with division facts through review and assessment.
	Practice and apply multidigit addition in varied contexts.	Practice and apply multidigit subtraction in varied contexts.	Review paper-and-pencil procedures. Practice and apply multiplication in varied contexts.	Develop paper-and-pencil procedures (1-digit and 2-digit divisors). Practice and apply division in varied contexts.

Table 1: *Math Facts and Whole-Number Operations Overview*

Addition and Subtraction Diagnosis and Review

Most work with math facts in Grade 4 focuses on practicing and assessing the multiplication and division facts. However, DPP items in Unit 1 provide an opportunity to assess students' fluency with the addition facts while DPP items in Unit 2 assess their fluency with the subtraction facts. Those students who exhibit reasonable fluency with the addition and subtraction facts will continue to practice these facts throughout the year as they engage in labs, activities, and games, and as they solve items in the Daily Practice and Problems and Home Practice.

The Addition and Subtraction Math Facts Review in Section 8 provides practice activities for students who require further work with the addition and subtraction math facts. Students can use the suggested activities, games, and flash cards at home with family members. This work should be distributed over time, rather than given all at once. While working with the addition and subtraction facts, students should continue with the rest of the class on the review and practice of the multiplication and division facts in the Daily Practice and Problems, Home Practice, and other lessons. They can use strategies, manipulatives, and calculators as they solve problems in class or at home.

An Overview of the Grade 4 Math Facts Program

Multiplication and Division Practice, Review, and Assessment

A yearlong, systematic, strategies-based review of the multiplication facts begins in Unit 3. Students review the multiplication facts in the same five groups as they studied them in third grade. They review each group of multiplication facts in the context of fact families, and in so doing, they begin to learn the related division facts. In Units 9–16, students concentrate on the division facts. See Table 2 for the sequence in which the groups will be reviewed and assessed. For a detailed explanation of our approach to learning and assessing the facts, see the TIMS Tutor: *Math Facts* in Section 3 of this book or in Section 9 of the *Teacher Implementation Guide.*

Unit	Review, Practice, and Assessment of the Math Facts Groups
1	Addition assessment
2	Subtraction assessment
3	Review the multiplication facts and study the division facts for the 5s and 10s Quiz on the multiplication facts for the 5s and 10s
4	Review the multiplication facts and study the division facts for the 2s and 3s Quiz on the multiplication facts for the 2s and 3s
5	Review the multiplication facts and study the division facts for the Square Numbers Quiz on the multiplication facts for the Square Numbers
6	Review the multiplication facts and study the division facts for the 9s Quiz on the multiplication facts for the 9s
7	Review the multiplication facts and study the division facts for the Last Six Facts Quiz on the multiplication facts for the Last Six Facts $(4 \times 6, 4 \times 7, 4 \times 8, 6 \times 7, 6 \times 8, 7 \times 8)$
8	Review the multiplication facts and study the division facts for all five groups Multiplication Facts Inventory Test Begin practice of the division facts for the 5s and 10s
9	Practice and assess the division facts for the 5s and 10s Quiz on the division facts for the 5s and 10s
10	Practice and assess the division facts for the 2s and 3s Quiz on the division facts for the 2s and 3s
11	Practice and assess the division facts for the Square Numbers Quiz on the division facts for the Square Numbers
12	Practice and assess the division facts for the 9s Quiz on the division facts for the 9s
13	Practice and assess the division facts for the Last Six Facts Quiz on the division facts for the Last Six Facts
14	Review and assess the division facts for the 2s, 5s, 10s, and the Square Numbers Quiz on the division facts for the 2s, 5s, 10s, and the Square Numbers
15	Review and assess the division facts for the 3s, 9s, and the Last Six Facts Quiz on the division facts for the 3s, 9s, and the Last Six Facts
16	Review all five division facts groups Division Facts Inventory Test

Table 2: *Math Facts Groups*

Launching the Study of the Multiplication and Division Facts. Unit 3
Lesson 1 *Multiplying and Dividing by 5s and 10s* sets up the math facts
strand in Grade 4:

- In Part 1 of Lesson 1, students learn to work with fact families to review
  the multiplication facts and study the division facts for the fives and tens.

- In Part 2, students investigate multiplication by zero and one.

- In Part 3, students quiz each other on the multiplication facts for the
  fives and tens. They use *Triangle Flash Cards* to assess themselves on
  the facts. They sort the cards into three piles: those they can answer
  quickly; those they can figure out with a strategy; and those that they
  need to learn. They begin a record of their current progress with the
  multiplication facts for the fives and tens by using a self-assessment
  page called the *Multiplication Facts I Know* chart. They circle the
  multiplication facts they know and can answer quickly. The chart is
  updated throughout Units 3–8.

After completing Lesson 1, students continue to practice the facts for the
fives and tens by completing various DPP items. Near the end of the unit, a
DPP item includes a quiz on the multiplication facts for the fives and tens.
Students take the quiz and update their *Multiplication Facts I Know* charts.

Math Facts in the Daily Practice and Problems for Units 4–16. Students
practice the multiplication and division facts as they use them to solve
problems in labs, activities, and games. However, the systematic practice and
assessment of the math facts takes place primarily in the DPP. The study of
the math facts in the DPP for Units 4–7 parallels the process in Unit 3:

- A DPP item instructs students to quiz each other on a group of multiplication facts using *Triangle Flash Cards.* Students sort the cards
  into three piles as described above. They update their *Multiplication
  Facts I Know* charts.

- Additional DPP items provide practice with the multiplication and
  division fact families for a particular group.

- Finally, a DPP item quizzes students on the multiplication facts for the
  given group. Students update their *Multiplication Facts I Know* charts.

The DPP for Unit 8 reviews all five groups of facts. A final DPP item in
Unit 8 includes an inventory test on the multiplication facts from all five
groups. Lesson 8 of Unit 8 begins the systematic study of the division facts.

The DPP in Units 9–16 repeat the process described above for the division
facts.

Using the Facts Resource Guide

As indicated above, the *Math Trailblazers* program for teaching math facts in Grade 4 is based upon a distributed study of the facts, located largely in the Daily Practice and Problems for each unit. The orderly distribution of the facts becomes disrupted if the pacing of the program is altered from the recommended schedule. The *Grade 4 Facts Resource Guide* provides a schedule for the study and assessment of math facts for teachers who find themselves using significantly more than the estimated number of class sessions assigned per unit. (If you do not fall behind the recommended schedule, there is no need for you to use the *Grade 4 Facts Resource Guide*—simply follow the math facts program as indicated in the units.)

The *Grade 4 Facts Resource Guide* translates the math facts program into a week-by-week calendar that roughly approximates the schedule for study of math facts that a class would follow if they remained close to the designated schedule for *Math Trailblazers* lessons. (See the Math Facts Calendar in Section 4.) In this manner, students will review all of the math facts for their particular grade even if they do not complete all of the units for the year.

This program is based on research that states that students learn the facts better using a strategies-based approach accompanied by distributed practice of small groups of facts. Therefore, we strongly recommend against using the math facts program in a shorter amount of time. The program can be tailored to the needs of individual students using the *Multiplication* and *Division Facts I Know* charts. Those students who know the facts based on the *Triangle Flash Cards* self-assessment will not need much practice. Other students will find that they only need to study one or two facts in a group. Still others will need to work on more facts, using the flash cards and games at home.

It is important to note that in *Math Trailblazers* much of the work for gaining fluency with math facts arises naturally in the problem-solving activities completed in class and in the homework. Thus, the math facts items included in the *Grade 4 Facts Resource Guide* do not reflect the full scope of the math facts program in the *Math Trailblazers* curriculum.

Resources

Isaacs, A.C., and W.M. Carroll. "Strategies for Basic Facts Instruction." *Teaching Children Mathematics,* 5 May, pp. 508–15, 1999.

National Research Council. "Developing Proficiency with Whole Numbers." In *Adding It Up: Helping Children Learn Mathematics,* J. Kilpatrick, J. Swafford, and B. Findell, eds. National Academy Press, Washington, DC, 2001.

Principles and Standards for School Mathematics. National Council of Teachers of Mathematics, Reston, VA, 2000.

Thornton, C.A. "Strategies for the Basic Facts." In J.N. Payne (ed.), *Mathematics for the Young Child.* National Council of Teachers of Mathematics, Reston, VA, 1990.

Information for Parents: Math Facts Philosophy

To inform parents about the curriculum's goals and philosophy of learning and assessing the math facts, send home a copy of the *Grade 4 Math Facts Philosophy* that immediately follows. This document is also available in the Unit 3 *Unit Resource Guide* immediately following the Background and on the *Teacher Resource CD*. A Spanish translation is available in Section 14 of the *Teacher Implementation Guide* and in the Letter Home: Spanish Translation Section in the *Unit Resource Guide File*.

INFORMATION FOR PARENTS

Grade 4 Math Facts Philosophy

The goal of the math facts strand in *Math Trailblazers* is for students to learn the basic facts efficiently, gain fluency with their use, and retain that fluency over time. A large body of research supports an approach that is built on a foundation of work with strategies and concepts. This not only leads to more effective learning and better retention, but also leads to development of mental math skills. Therefore, the teaching of the basic facts in *Math Trailblazers* is characterized by the following elements:

Use of Strategies. Students first approach the basic facts as problems to be solved rather than as facts to be memorized. We encourage the use of strategies to find facts, so students become confident that they can find answers to fact problems that they do not immediately recall. In this way, students learn that math is more than memorizing facts and rules which "you either get or you don't."

Distributed Facts Practice. Students study small groups of facts that can be found using similar strategies. In fourth grade, the multiplication and division facts are divided into five groups. During the first semester students review the multiplication facts and develop strategies for the division facts, one group at a time. During the second semester, they review and practice the division facts in each group so that they can develop fluency with all of the facts by the end of the year. Practice of the five groups of facts is distributed throughout the curriculum and students are also given flash cards to practice groups of facts at home.

Practice in Context. Students learn the facts as they use them to solve problems in the labs, activities, and games.

Appropriate Assessment. Students are regularly assessed to determine whether they can find answers to fact problems quickly and accurately and whether they can retain this skill over time. A short quiz follows the study and review of each group of facts. Each student records his or her progress on *Facts I Know* charts and determines which facts he or she needs to study.

A Multiyear Approach. In Grades 1 and 2, the curriculum emphasizes the use of strategies that enable students to develop fluency with the addition and subtraction facts by the end of second grade. In Grade 3, they review the subtraction facts and begin strategy work with multiplication facts in order to achieve fluency by the end of the year. In Grade 4, the addition and subtraction facts are checked, the multiplication facts are reviewed, and fluency with the division facts is achieved. In Grade 5 all facts continue to be reviewed so as to retain fluency.

Facts Will Not Act as Gatekeepers. Use of strategies, calculators, and printed multiplication tables allows students to continue to work on interesting problems and experiments while they are learning the facts. Students are not prevented from learning more complex mathematics because they cannot perform well on facts tests.

TIMS Tutor: *Math Facts*

The TIMS Tutor: *Math Facts* provides an in-depth exploration of the math facts concepts and ideas behind the math facts strand in *Math Trailblazers*. This document also appears in Section 9 TIMS Tutors in the *Teacher Implementation Guide*.

Students need to learn the math facts. Estimation, mental arithmetic, checking the reasonableness of results, and paper-and-pencil calculations require the ability to give quick, accurate responses when using basic facts. The question is not if students should learn the math facts, but how. Which teaching methods are most efficient and effective? To answer this question, the authors of *Math Trailblazers* drew upon educational research and their own classroom experiences to develop a comprehensive plan for teaching the math facts.

Philosophy

The goal of the *Math Trailblazers* math facts strand is for students to learn the basic facts efficiently, gain fluency with their use, and retain that fluency over time. A large body of research supports an approach that is built on a foundation of work with strategies and concepts. This not only leads to more effective learning and better retention, it also leads to development of mental math skills. Therefore, the teaching and assessment of the basic facts in *Math Trailblazers* is characterized by the following elements:

- *Early emphasis on problem solving.* Students first approach the basic facts as problems to be solved rather than as facts to be memorized. Students invent their own strategies to solve these problems or learn appropriate strategies from others through class discussion. Students' natural strategies, especially counting strategies, are explicitly encouraged. In this way, students learn that math is more than memorizing facts and rules that "you either get or you don't."

- *De-emphasis of rote work.* Fluency with the math facts is an important component of any student's mathematical learning. Research has shown that an overemphasis on memorization and the frequent administration of timed tests are counterproductive. Both of these can produce undesirable results (Isaacs and Carroll, 1999; Van de Walle, 2001; National Research Council, 2001). We encourage the use of strategies to find facts, so students become confident they can find answers to fact problems that they do not immediately recall.

- *Gradual and systematic introduction of facts.* Students study the facts in small groups that can be solved using similar strategies. Students first work on simple strategies for easy facts and then progress to more sophisticated strategies and harder facts. By the end of the process, they gain fluency with all required facts.

- *Ongoing practice.* Work on the math facts is distributed throughout the curriculum, especially in the Daily Practice and Problems (DPP), Home Practice, and games. This practice for fluency, however, takes place only after students have a conceptual understanding of the operations and have achieved proficiency with strategies for solving basic fact problems. Delaying practice in this way means that less practice is required to achieve fluency.

- *Appropriate assessment.* Teachers assess students' knowledge of the facts through observations as they work on activities, labs, and games as well as through the appropriate use of written tests and quizzes. Beginning in first grade, periodic, short quizzes in the DPP naturally follow the study of small groups of facts organized around specific strategies. As self-assessment in Grades 3–5, each student records his or her progress on *Facts I Know* charts and determines which facts he or she needs to study. Inventory tests of all facts for each operation are used sparingly in Grades 2–5 (no more than twice per year) to assess students' progress with fact fluency. The goal of the math facts assessment program is to determine the degree to which students can find answers to fact problems quickly and accurately and whether they can retain this skill over time.

- *Multiyear approach.* In Grades 1 and 2, *Math Trailblazers* emphasizes strategies that lead to fluency with the addition and subtraction facts. In Grade 3, students gain fluency with the multiplication facts while reviewing the addition and subtraction facts. In Grade 4, students achieve fluency with the division facts and verify fluency with the multiplication facts. In Grade 5, the multiplication and division facts are systematically reviewed and assessed.

- *Facts are not gatekeepers.* Students are not prevented from learning more complex mathematics because they do not perform well on fact tests. Use of strategies, calculators, and other math tools (e.g., manipulatives, hundred charts, printed multiplication tables) allows students to continue to work on interesting problems while they are still learning the facts.

The following goals for the math facts are consistent with the recommendations in the National Council of Teachers of Mathematics *Principles and Standards for School Mathematics:*

Expectations by Grade Level

- In kindergarten, students use manipulatives and invent their own strategies to solve addition and subtraction problems.
- By the end of first grade, all students can solve all basic addition and subtraction problems using some strategy. Fluency is not emphasized; strategies are. Some work with beginning concepts of multiplication takes place.
- In second grade, learning efficient strategies for addition and especially subtraction continues to be emphasized. Work with multiplication concepts continues. By the end of the year, students are expected to demonstrate fluency with all the addition and subtraction facts.
- In third grade, students review the subtraction facts. They develop efficient strategies for learning the multiplication facts and demonstrate fluency with the multiplication facts.
- In fourth grade, students review the multiplication facts and develop strategies for the division facts. By the end of the year, we expect fluency with all the division facts.
- In fifth grade, students review the multiplication and division facts and are expected to maintain fluency with all the facts.

This is summarized in the following chart:

Grade	Addition	Subtraction	Multiplication	Division
K	• invented strategies	• invented strategies		
1	• strategies	• strategies		
2	• strategies • practice leading to fluency	• strategies • practice leading to fluency		
3	• review and practice	• review and practice	• strategies • practice leading to fluency	
4	• assessment and remediation as required	• assessment and remediation as required	• review and practice	• strategies • practice leading to fluency
5	• assessment and remediation as required	• assessment and remediation as required	• review and practice	• review and practice

Table 1: *Math Facts Scope and Sequence*

Strategies for Learning the Facts

Students are encouraged to learn the math facts by first employing a variety of strategies. Concepts and skills are learned more easily and are retained longer if they are meaningful. By first concentrating on concepts and strategies, we increase retention and reduce the amount of time necessary for rote memorization. Researchers note that over time, students develop techniques that are increasingly sophisticated and efficient. Experience with the strategies provides a basis for understanding the operation involved and for gaining fluency with the facts. In this section, we describe possible strategies for learning the addition, subtraction, multiplication, and division facts. The strategies for each operation are listed roughly in order of increasing sophistication.

Strategies for Addition Facts

Common strategies include counting all, counting on, doubles, making or using 10, and reasoning from known facts.

Counting All

This is a particularly straightforward strategy. For example, to solve 7 + 8, the student gets 7 of something and 8 of something and counts how many there are altogether. The "something" could be beans or chips or marks on paper. In any case, the student counts all the objects to find the sum. This is perhaps not a very efficient method, but it is effective, especially for small numbers, and is usually well understood by the student.

Counting On

This is a natural strategy, particularly for adding 1, 2, or 3. Counters such as beans or chips may or may not be used. As an example with counters, consider 8 + 3. The student gets 8 beans, and then 3 more, but instead of counting the first 8 again, she simply counts the 3 added beans: "9, 10, 11."

Even if counters are not used, finger gestures can help keep track of how many more have been counted on. For example, to solve 8 + 3, the student counts "9, 10, 11," holding up a finger each time a number word is said; when three fingers are up, the last word said is the answer.

Doubles

Facts such as 4 + 4 = 8 are easier to remember than facts with two different addends. Some visual imagery can help, too: two hands for 5 + 5, a carton of eggs for 6 + 6, a calendar for 7 + 7, and so on.

Making a 10

Facts with a sum of 10, such as 7 + 3 and 6 + 4, are also easier to remember than other facts. Ten frames can create visual images of making a 10. For example, 8 is shown in a ten frame like the one in Figure 1:

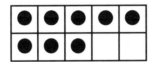

Figure 1: *A ten frame*

This visual imagery helps students remember, for example, that 8 + 2 = 10.

Using a 10

Students who are comfortable partitioning and combining small numbers can use that knowledge to find the sums of larger numbers. In particular, there are many strategies that involve using the number 10. For example, to find 9 + 7, we can decompose 7 into 1 + 6 and then 9 + 7 = 9 + 1 + 6 = 10 + 6 = 16. Similarly, 8 + 7 = 8 + 2 + 5 = 10 + 5 = 15.

Reasoning from Known Facts

If you know what 7 + 7 is, then 7 + 8 is not much harder: it's just 1 more. So, the "near doubles" can be derived from knowing the doubles.

Strategies for Subtraction Facts

Common strategies for subtraction include using counters, counting up, counting back, using 10, and reasoning from related addition and subtraction facts.

Using Counters

This method consists of modeling the problem with counters like beans or chips. For example, to solve 8 − 3, the student gets 8 beans, removes 3 beans, and counts the remaining beans to find the difference. As with using the addition strategy "counting all," this is a relatively straightforward strategy that may not be efficient but has the great advantage of usually being well understood by the student.

Counting Up

The student starts at the lower number and counts on to the higher number, perhaps using fingers to keep track of how many numbers are counted. For example, to solve $8 - 5$, the student wants to know how to get from 5 to 8 and counts up 3 numbers: 6, 7, 8. So, $8 - 5 = 3$.

$8 - 5 = 3$

5 6 7 8

Figure 2: *Counting up*

Counting Back

Counting back works best for subtracting 1, 2, or 3. For larger numbers, it is probably best to count up. For example, to solve $9 - 2$, the student counts back 2 numbers: 8, 7. So, $9 - 2 = 7$.

$9 - 2 = 7$ 9 8 7

Figure 3: *Counting back*

Using a 10

Students follow the pattern they find when subtracting 10, e.g., $17 - 10 = 7$ and $13 - 10 = 3$, to learn close facts, e.g., $17 - 9 = 8$ and $13 - 9 = 4$. Since $17 - 9$ will be 1 more than $17 - 10$, they can reason that the answer will be 8, or $7 + 1$.

Making a 10

Knowing the addition facts which have a sum of 10, e.g., $6 + 4 = 10$, can be helpful in finding differences from 10, e.g., $10 - 6 = 4$ and $10 - 4 = 6$. Students can use ten frames to visualize these problems as shown in Figure 4. These facts can then also be used to find close facts, such as $11 - 4 = 7$.

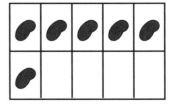

$10 - 4 = 6$

Figure 4: *Using a ten frame*

Using Doubles

The addition doubles, e.g., $8 + 8 = 16$ and $6 + 6 = 12$, can be used to learn the subtraction "half-doubles" as well: $16 - 8 = 8$ and $12 - 6 = 6$. These facts can then be used to figure out close facts, such as $13 - 6 = 7$ and $15 - 8 = 7$.

Reasoning from Related Addition and Subtraction Facts

Knowing that $8 + 7 = 15$ would seem to be of some help in solving $15 - 7$. Unfortunately, however, knowing related addition facts may not be so helpful to younger or less mathematically mature students. Nevertheless, reasoning from known facts is a powerful strategy for those who can apply it and should be encouraged.

Strategies for Multiplication Facts

Common strategies for multiplication include skip counting, counting up or down from a known fact, doubling, breaking a product into the sum of known products, and using patterns.

Skip Counting

Students begin skip counting and solving problems informally that involve multiplicative situations in first grade. By the time formal work with the multiplication facts is begun in third grade, they should be fairly proficient with skip counting. This strategy is particularly useful for facts such as the 2s, 3s, 5s, and 10s, for which skip counting is easy.

Counting Up or Down from a Known Fact

This strategy involves skip counting forward once or twice from a known fact. For example, if a child knows that 5×5 is 25, then this can be used to solve 6×5 (5 more) or 4×5 (5 less). Some children use this for harder facts. For 7×6, they can use the fact that $5 \times 6 = 30$ as a starting point and then count on by sixes to 42.

Doubling

Some children use doubling relationships to help them with multiplication facts involving 4, 6, and 8. For example, 4×7 is twice as much as 2×7. Since $2 \times 7 = 14$, it follows that 4×7 is 28. Since 3×8 is 24, it follows that 6×8 is 48.

Breaking a Product into the Sum of Known Products

A fact like 7×8 can be broken into the sum $5 \times 8 + 2 \times 8$ since $7 = 5 + 2$. (See Figure 5.) The previous two strategies are special cases of this more general strategy.

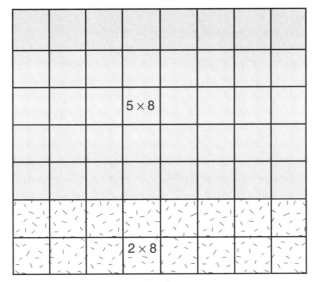

$$7 \times 8 =$$
$$5 \times 8 + 2 \times 8 =$$
$$40 + 16 = 56$$

Figure 5: *Breaking up 7×8*

Patterns

A. Perhaps the best-known examples of patterns are the nines patterns:

   1. When the nines products are listed in a column, as shown below, it is easy to see that the digits in the tens place count up by one (0, 1, 2, 3, . . .) and that the digits in the ones place count down by one (9, 8, 7, . . .).

      9
      18
      27
      36
      45
      54
      63
      72
      81

   2. The sums of the two digits in each of the nines products above are all equal to nine. For example, the sum of the digits in 36 is $3 + 6 = 9$; the sum of the digits in 72 is $7 + 2 = 9$. Adding the digits of a number to see whether they add up to nine can be a strategy in remembering a nines fact. For example, a student might think, "Let me see, does 9×6 equal 54 or 56? It must be 54 since $5 + 4$ is 9, but $5 + 6$ is not 9."

   3. The digit in the tens place in a nines fact is one less than the number being multiplied. For example, $4 \times 9 = 36$, and 3 is one less than 4. This can be combined with the previous pattern to derive nines facts. For example, 3×9 is in the twenties. Since $2 + 7$ is 9, 3×9 must be 27.

   4. Nines can easily be computed using the counting down strategy. Nine times a digit is the same as 10 times the digit, minus the digit. For example, 9×6 is $10 \times 6 - 6 = 54$

B. Other patterns.

   There are other patterns that can be useful in remembering other special facts:

   1. 0 times a number equals 0.
   2. 1 times a number equals the number.
   3. 2 times a number is double the number.
   4. 5 times a number ends in 0 or 5; even numbers times 5 end in 0 and odd numbers times five end in 5.
   5. 10 times a number is the same number with a 0 on the end.

Sequencing the Study of Multiplication Facts

In kindergarten, children solve word problems involving multiplication situations. Beginning in first grade, the curriculum develops a conceptual foundation for multiplication through a variety of multiplication models, including repeated addition, the array model, and the number-line model. Fluency with the multiplication facts is expected by the end of third grade. Strategies are often introduced in specific, third-grade lessons. Practice is continued in subsequent lessons and especially in the Daily Practice and Problems and Home Practice. We do not introduce the multiplication facts in the order in which they are traditionally taught (first learning the 2s, then the

3s, then the 4s, etc.). Rather, we emphasize thinking strategies for the facts, introducing fact groups in the following order:

2s, 3s, 5s, and 10s. The 2s, 3s, 5s, and 10s are easily solved using skip counting.

Square numbers such as $3 \times 3 = 9$, $4 \times 4 = 16$, and $5 \times 5 = 25$. These are introduced by arranging tiles into square arrays.

Nines. Students explore patterns for nines.

Last six facts. After students have learned the facts listed above and their turn-around facts ($9 \times 6 = 6 \times 9$), there are only six more facts to learn: 4×6, 4×7, 4×8, 6×7, 6×8, and 7×8.

Strategies for Division Facts

The main strategy for learning the division facts is to think of the related multiplication fact. Therefore, students review the multiplication facts and develop fluency with the division facts by working with fact families. (Fact families are groups of related facts. An example of a fact family is $3 \times 4 = 12$, $4 \times 3 = 12$, $12 \div 3 = 4$, and $12 \div 4 = 3$.)

Using the Right Strategy

Different strategies appeal to different students. Students should not feel overburdened with the need to determine which is the "correct" strategy for a given fact. We do not intend to give them a new layer of things to learn. For example, when asked to explain a strategy for a fact, a student may say, "I've used it so much that now I just remember it." "Just remembering" is obviously an efficient strategy. The purpose of suggesting and discussing various strategies is to give students other, perhaps helpful, ways of learning the facts and to give them the confidence to think problems through when necessary. Students should have the opportunity to choose the strategies that work best for them or to invent their own.

The *Math Trailblazers* math facts program pervades most of the curriculum's components. Work with math facts can be found in different kinds of lessons. These are described in this section.

Math Facts Lessons

Figure 6: *Discussing fact strategies*

As students work on problems in the labs and activities, they should be encouraged to use and to discuss various strategies for solving math facts problems.

Everyday Work

As students work on problems in the labs and activities, they should be encouraged to use and to discuss various strategies for solving math facts problems. A number of important goals can best be reached through such discussions.

One goal is to legitimize all valid strategies, even those that may be less efficient. When students see their intuitive methods recognized and validated, they tend to perceive mathematical knowledge as continuous with everyday knowledge and common sense. We thus hope to avoid the unfortunate tendency of many students to separate their knowledge of mathematics from their knowledge of the real world.

By discussing strategies as they arise in context, students and teachers can explore how the strategies work and can verify that they are being used properly. Students should come to realize that a fact strategy that gives wrong answers is not very useful.

A second goal of our approach is to encourage students to communicate mathematical ideas. There are several reasons to stress communication: Students can learn from one another; communicating a method requires higher orders of thinking than simply applying that method; and skill at communicating is important in itself. We are social creatures. Mathematics and science are social endeavors in which communication is crucial.

A third goal of encouraging discussions of various methods is to give the teacher opportunities to learn about how students think. Knowing more about students' thinking helps the teacher ask better questions and plan more effective lessons.

Strategy Lessons

We feel that occasionally it is appropriate for lessons to focus on certain strategies that are developmentally appropriate for most students. Our plan is to begin with simple strategies that should be accessible to all students and to progress gradually to more complex forms of reasoning. For example, in the fall of first grade, we have several lessons that stress counting on to solve certain addition problems. Later, we explicitly introduce making a 10 and other, more sophisticated, strategies.

In general, you should expect your students to come up with effective strategies on their own. Our strategy lessons are intended to explore how and why various strategies work and also to codify and organize the strategies the students invent. They are not meant to dictate the only appropriate strategy for a given problem or to discourage students from using strategies they understand and like. They should be seen as opportunities to discuss strategies that may be appropriate for many students and to encourage their wider use.

Our ultimate goal is to produce students who can think mathematically, who can solve problems and deal easily with quantified information, and who enjoy mathematics and are not afraid of it. It is easier to do all of the above if one has fluency with the basic math facts. Practice strengthens students' abilities to use strategies and moves students toward fluency with the facts. Practice that follows instruction that stresses the use of strategies has been shown to improve students' fluency with the math facts. We recommend, and have incorporated into the curriculum, the following practice to gain this fluency.

Practice in Context
The primary practice of math facts will arise naturally for the students as they participate in the labs and other activities in the curriculum. These labs and activities offer many opportunities to practice addition, subtraction, multiplication, and division in a meaningful way. The lessons involve the student visually with drawings and patterns, auditorily through discussion, and tactilely through the use of many tools such as manipulatives and calculators.

Pages of problems on the basic facts are not only unnecessary, they can be counterproductive. Students may come to regard mathematics as mostly memorization and may perceive it as meaningless and unconnected to their everyday lives.

Structured Practice
Student-friendly, structured practice is built into the curriculum, especially in the DPP, Home Practice, and games. One small group of related math facts is presented to the students at a time. The practice of groups of facts is carefully distributed throughout the year. A small set of facts grouped in a meaningful way leads students to develop strategies such as adding doubles, counting back, or using a 10 for dealing with a particular situation. Furthermore, a small set of facts is a manageable amount to learn and remember.

Beginning in the second half of first grade and continuing through fifth grade, a small group of facts to be studied in a unit is introduced in the DPP. Through DPP items, students practice the facts and take a short assessment. Beginning in second grade, students use flash cards for additional practice with specific groups of facts. Facts are also practiced in many word problems in the DPP, Home Practice, and individual lessons. These problems allow students to focus on other interesting mathematical ideas as they also gain more fact practice.

Games
A variety of games are included in the curriculum, both in the lessons and in the DPP items of many units. A summary of the games used in a particular grade can be found in Section 12 of the *Teacher Implementation Guide.* Once students learn the rules of the games, they should play them periodically in class and at home for homework. Games provide an opportunity to encourage family involvement in the math program. When a game is assigned for homework, a note can be sent home with a place for the family members to sign, affirming that they played the game with their student.

Practice

Our ultimate goal is to produce students who can think mathematically, who can solve problems and deal easily with quantified information, and who enjoy mathematics and are not afraid of it. It is easier to do all of the above if one has fluency with the basic math facts.

Figure 7: *Playing a game*

Use of Calculators

The relationship between knowing the math facts and the use of calculators is an interesting one. Using a multiplication table or a calculator when necessary to find a fact helps promote familiarity and reinforces the math facts. Students soon figure out that it is quicker and more efficient to know the basic facts than to have to use these tools. The use of calculators also requires excellent estimation skills so that one can easily check for errors in calculator computations. Rather than eliminating the need for fluency with the facts, successful calculator use for solving complex problems depends on fact knowledge.

When to Practice

Practicing small groups of facts often for short periods of time is more effective than practicing many facts less often for long periods of time. For example, practicing 8 to 10 subtraction facts for 5 minutes several times a week is better than practicing all the subtraction facts for half an hour once a week. Good times for practicing the facts for 5 or 10 minutes during the school day include the beginning of the day, the beginning of math class, when students have completed an assignment, when an impending activity is delayed, or when an activity ends earlier than expected. Practicing small groups of facts at home involves parents in the process and frees class time for more interesting mathematics.

Practicing small groups of facts often for short periods of time is more effective than practicing many facts less often for long periods of time.

Assessment

Throughout the curriculum, teachers assess students' knowledge of the facts through observations as they work on activities, labs, and games. In Grades 3–5, students can use their *Facts I Know* charts to record their own progress in learning the facts. This type of self-assessment is very important in helping each student to become responsible for his or her own learning. Students are able to personalize their study of facts and not waste valuable time studying facts they already know.

In the second half of first grade, a sequence of facts assessments is provided in the Daily Practice and Problems. A more comprehensive facts assessment program begins in second grade. This program assesses students' progress in learning the facts, as outlined in the Expectations by Grade Level section of this tutor. As students develop strategies for a given group of facts, short quizzes accompany the practice. Students know which facts will be tested, focus practice in class and at home on those facts, then take the quiz. As they take the quiz, they use one color pencil to write answers before a given time limit, then use another color to complete the problems they need more time to answer. Students then use their *Facts I Know* charts to make a record of those facts they answered quickly, those facts they answered correctly but with less efficient strategies, and those facts they did not know at all. Using this information, students can concentrate their efforts on gaining fluency with those facts they answered correctly, but not quickly. They also know to develop strategies for those facts they could not answer at all. In this way, the number of facts studied at any one time becomes more manageable, practice becomes more meaningful, and the process less intimidating.

Tests of all the facts for any operation have a very limited role. They are used no more than two times a year to show growth over time and should not be given daily or weekly. Since we rarely, if ever, need to recall 100 facts at one time in everyday life, overemphasizing tests of all the facts reinforces the notion that math is nothing more than rote memorization and has no connection to the real world. Quizzes of small numbers of facts are as effective and not as threatening. They give students, parents, and teachers the information needed to continue learning and practicing efficiently. With an assessment approach based on strategies and the use of small groups of facts, students can see mathematics as connected to their own thinking and gain confidence in their mathematical abilities.

Conclusion

Research provides clear indications for curriculum developers and teachers about the design of effective math facts instruction. These recommendations formed the foundation of the *Math Trailblazers* math facts program. Developing strategies for learning the facts (rather than relying on rote memorization), distributing practice of small groups of facts, applying math facts in interesting problems, and using an appropriate assessment program—all are consistent with recommendations from current research. It is an instructional approach that encourages students to make sense of the mathematics they are learning. The resulting program will add efficiency and effectiveness to your students' learning of the math facts.

References

Ashlock, R.B., and C.A. Washbon. "Games: Practice Activities for the Basic Facts." In M.N. Suydam and R.E. Reys (eds.), *Developing Computational Skills: 1978 Yearbook.* National Council of Teachers of Mathematics, Reston, VA, 1978.

Beattie, L.D. "Children's Strategies for Solving Subtraction-Fact Combinations." *Arithmetic Teacher,* 27 (1), pp. 14–15, 1979.

Brownell, W.A., and C.B. Chazal. "The Effects of Premature Drill in Third-Grade Arithmetic." *Journal of Educational Research,* 29 (1), 1935.

Carpenter, T.P., and J.M. Moser. "The Acquisition of Addition and Subtraction Concepts in Grades One through Three." *Journal for Research in Mathematics Education,* 15 (3), pp. 179–202, 1984.

Cook, C.J., and J.A. Dossey. "Basic Fact Thinking Strategies for Multiplication—Revisited." *Journal for Research in Mathematics Education,* 13 (3), pp. 163–171, 1982.

Davis, E.J. "Suggestions for Teaching the Basic Facts of Arithmetic." In M.N. Suydam and R.E. Reys (eds.), *Developing Computational Skills: 1978 Yearbook.* National Council of Teachers of Mathematics, Reston, VA, 1978.

Fuson, K.C. "Teaching Addition, Subtraction, and Place-Value Concepts." In L. Wirszup and R. Streit (eds.), *Proceedings of the UCSMP International Conference on Mathematics Education: Developments in School Mathematics Education Around the World: Applications-Oriented Curricula and Technology-Supported Learning for All Students.* National Council of Teachers of Mathematics, Reston, VA, 1987.

Fuson, K.C., J.W. Stigler, and K. Bartsch. "Grade Placement of Addition and Subtraction Topics in Japan, Mainland China, the Soviet Union, Taiwan, and the United States." *Journal for Research in Mathematics Education,* 19 (5), pp. 449–456, 1988.

Fuson, K.C., and G.B. Willis. "Subtracting by Counting Up: More Evidence." *Journal for Research in Mathematics Education,* 19 (5), pp. 402–420, 1988.

Greer, B. "Multiplication and Division as Models of Situations." In D.A. Grouws (ed.), *Handbook of Research on Mathematics Teaching and Learning: A Project of the National Council of Teachers of Mathematics* (Chapter 13). Macmillan, New York, 1992.

Hiebert, James. "Relationships between Research and the NCTM Standards." *Journal for Research in Mathematics Education,* 30 January, pp. 3–19, 1999.

Isaacs, A.C., and W.M. Carroll. "Strategies for Basic Facts Instruction." *Teaching Children Mathematics,* 5 May, pp. 508–515, 1999.

Kouba, V.L., C.A. Brown, T.P. Carpenter, M.M. Lindquist, E.A. Silver, and J.O. Swafford. "Results of the Fourth NAEP Assessment of Mathematics: Number, Operations, and Word Problems." *Arithmetic Teacher,* 35 (8), pp. 14–19, 1988.

Myers, A.C., and C.A. Thornton. "The Learning-Disabled Child—Learning the Basic Facts." *Arithmetic Teacher,* 25 (3), pp. 46–50, 1977.

National Research Council. "Developing Proficiency with Whole Numbers." In J. Kilpatrick, J. Swafford, and B. Findell (eds.), *Adding It Up: Helping Children Learn Mathematics,* pp. 181–230. National Academy Press, Washington, DC, 2001.

Principles and Standards for School Mathematics. National Council of Teachers of Mathematics, Reston, VA, 2000.

Rathmell, E.C. "Using Thinking Strategies to Teach the Basic Facts." In M.N. Suydam and R.E. Reys (eds.), *Developing Computational Skills: 1978 Yearbook.* National Council of Teachers of Mathematics, Reston, VA, 1978.

Rathmell, E.C., and P.R. Trafton. "Whole Number Computation." In J.N. Payne (ed.), *Mathematics for the Young Child.* National Council of Teachers of Mathematics, Reston, VA, 1990.

Swart, W.L. "Some Findings on Conceptual Development of Computational Skills." *Arithmetic Teacher,* 32 (5), pp. 36–38, 1985.

Thornton, C.A. "Doubles Up—Easy!" *Arithmetic Teacher,* 29 (8), p. 20, 1982.

Thornton, C.A. "Emphasizing Thinking Strategies in Basic Fact Instruction." *Journal for Research in Mathematics Education,* 9 (3), pp. 214–227, 1978.

Thornton, C.A. "Solution Strategies: Subtraction Number Facts." *Educational Studies in Mathematics,* 21 (1), pp. 241–263, 1990.

Thornton, C.A. "Strategies for the Basic Facts." In J.N. Payne (ed.), *Mathematics for the Young Child.* National Council of Teachers of Mathematics, Reston, VA, 1990.

Thornton, C.A., and P.J. Smith. "Action Research: Strategies for Learning Subtraction Facts." *Arithmetic Teacher,* 35 (8), pp. 8–12, 1988.

Van de Walle, J. *Elementary and Middle School Mathematics: Teaching Developmentally.* Addison Wesley, New York, 2001.

Grade 4 Math Facts Calendar

The Grade 4 Math Facts Calendar outlines a schedule for math facts practice, review, and assessment that roughly follows the schedule in the Unit Outlines in the *Unit Resource Guides* and in Section 4 of the *Teacher Implementation Guide.* Classrooms that are moving significantly more slowly through the units than is recommended in the Unit Outlines can use this schedule for study of the math facts to ensure that students receive the complete math facts program.

All of the materials referenced in the Math Facts Calendar are located elsewhere in *Math Trailblazers* as well as in the *Grade 4 Facts Resource Guide.*

The elements included in the Math Facts Calendar are described below.

Math Facts Groups	Weeks	Daily Practice and Problems	Home Practice	Triangle Flash Cards	Facts Quizzes and Tests
Multiplication Review and Division Practice for the 5s and 10s	7–8	The lesson, *Multiplying and Dividing with 5s and 10s* (Unit 3 Lesson 1), begins the formal Grade 4 math facts program. Complete that lesson prior to beginning the DPP items listed below. Unit 3: Items 3B, 3C, 3E, 3F, 3H & 3K–3M	Unit 3 Parts 1, 4 & 5	*Triangle Flash Cards: 5s* and *10s*	DPP Item 3M is a quiz on the multiplication facts for the 5s and 10s. The *Multiplication Facts I Know* chart is updated.
Multiplication Review and Division Practice for the 2s and 3s	9–10	Unit 4: Items 4A–4C, 4E–4G, 4J–4M, 4R & 4S	Unit 4 Part 1	*Triangle Flash Cards: 2s* and *3s*	DPP Item 4S is a quiz on the 2s and 3s. The *Multiplication Facts I Know* chart is updated.

Math Facts Groups

The *Math Trailblazers* program for practicing, reviewing, and assessing the multiplication and division facts is organized into five groups of facts. This column describes which math facts are to be practiced, reviewed, and assessed.

Weeks

Week 1 in the schedule refers to the first week of school. Week 2 refers to the second week of school, and so on.

Daily Practice and Problems

The DPP items from each unit that focus on the math facts are listed in this column.

The Daily Practice and Problems (DPP) is a series of short exercises that:

- provide distributed practice in computation and a structure for systematic review of the basic math facts;
- develop concepts and skills such as number sense, mental math, telling time, and working with money throughout the year; and
- review topics, presenting concepts in new contexts and linking ideas from unit to unit.

There are three types of items: Bits, Tasks, and Challenges. Most are written so that they can be quickly copied onto the blackboard.

- Bits are short and should take no more than five or ten minutes to complete. They often provide practice with a skill or the basic math facts.
- Tasks take ten to fifteen minutes to complete.
- Challenges usually take longer than fifteen minutes to complete and the problems are more thought-provoking. They stretch students' problem-solving skills.

The DPP may be used in class for practice and review, as assessment, or for homework. Notes for teachers provide answers as well as suggestions for using the items. Only those DPP items that focus on the math facts are listed here.

For more information on the Daily Practice and Problems, see the Daily Practice and Problems and Home Practice Guide in the *Teacher Implementation Guide.*

Home Practice

The Home Practice is a series of problems, located in the *Discovery Assignment Book,* that are designed to be sent home with students to supplement homework assignments. Each Home Practice is divided into several parts that can be assigned separately. Part 1 of the Home Practice in each unit (beginning in Unit 3) recommends use of *Triangle Flash Cards* for practice of specific groups of facts. As part of the Home Practice assignments, students also update their *Facts I Know* charts.

For more information on the Home Practice, see the Daily Practice and Problems and Home Practice Guide in the *Teacher Implementation Guide.*

Triangle Flash Cards

As part of the DPP and Home Practice, fourth-grade students use the *Triangle Flash Cards* to practice and assess their knowledge of specific groups of math facts. Students categorize facts into three groups (facts I know quickly, facts I know using a strategy, and facts I need to learn). They record this information on a chart that is updated regularly.

The *Triangle Flash Cards* are distributed in Units 3–8 and 10–13 in the *Discovery Assignment Book.* Copies of the *Triangle Flash Cards* are also included in Section 7. The *Multiplication Facts I Know* chart is distributed in Unit 3 Lesson 1 in the *Discovery Assignment Book.* The *Division Facts I Know* chart is distributed in Unit 8 Lesson 8. These charts are reproduced in Section 5.

Facts Quizzes and Tests

Periodic quizzes of small groups of math facts are given as part of the DPP. Facts are grouped to encourage the use of strategies in learning facts. In fourth grade, a test on all the multiplication facts is given in Unit 8. A test on all the division facts is given in Unit 16.

Grade 4 Math Facts Calendar

Math Facts Groups	Weeks	Daily Practice and Problems	Home Practice	Triangle Flash Cards	Facts Quizzes and Tests
Addition and Subtraction Review	1–6	Unit 1: Items 1A–1E, 1K & 1M Unit 2: Items 2G–2I, 2M, 2O, 2Q, 2S & 2AA	Unit 1 Part 1 Unit 2 Parts 1 & 4		DPP Items 1K and 1M can serve as addition facts inventory tests. DPP Items 2M, 2O, 2Q, and 2S can serve as subtraction facts inventory tests.
Multiplication Review and Division Practice for the 5s and 10s	7–8	The lesson, *Multiplying and Dividing with 5s and 10s* (Unit 3 Lesson 1), begins the formal Grade 4 math facts program. Complete that lesson prior to beginning the DPP items listed below. Unit 3: Items 3B, 3C, 3E, 3F, 3H & 3K–3M	Unit 3 Parts 1, 4 & 5	*Triangle Flash Cards: 5s and 10s*	DPP Item 3M is a quiz on the multiplication facts for the 5s and 10s. The *Multiplication Facts I Know* chart is updated.
Multiplication Review and Division Practice for the 2s and 3s	9–10	Unit 4: Items 4A–4C, 4E–4G, 4J–4M, 4R & 4S	Unit 4 Part 1	*Triangle Flash Cards: 2s and 3s*	DPP Item 4S is a quiz on the 2s and 3s. The *Multiplication Facts I Know* chart is updated.
Multiplication Review and Division Practice for the Square Numbers	11–13	Unit 5: Items 5A, 5B, 5G–5J, 5L, 5N, 5P, 5T & 5U	Unit 5 Part 1	*Triangle Flash Cards: Square Numbers*	DPP Item 5U is a quiz on the square numbers. The *Multiplication Facts I Know* chart is updated.
Multiplication Review and Division Practice for the 9s	14–15	Unit 6: Items 6A, 6C, 6G, 6H, 6J–6M & 6O	Unit 6 Parts 1 & 2	*Triangle Flash Cards: 9s*	DPP Item 6O is a quiz on the 9s. The *Multiplication Facts I Know* chart is updated.

Grade 4 Math Facts Calendar *(continued)*

Math Facts Groups	Weeks	Daily Practice and Problems	Home Practice	Triangle Flash Cards	Facts Quizzes and Tests
Multiplication Review and Division Practice for The Last Six Facts	16–18	Unit 7: Items 7A, 7B, 7E–7H, 7J, 7M–7O, 7Y & 7AA	Unit 7 Parts 1 & 5	*Triangle Flash Cards: The Last Six Facts*	DPP Item 7AA is a quiz on The Last Six Facts. The *Multiplication Facts I Know* chart is updated.
Multiplication Assessment and Division Practice for All Fact Groups	19–20	Unit 8: Items 8A, 8E–8G, 8I, 8M, 8S, 8U & 8V The lesson *Facts I Know: Multiplication and Division Facts* (Unit 8 Lesson 8) begins the review and assessment of the division facts.	Unit 8 Part 1	*Triangle Flash Cards: 5s, 10s, 2s, 3s, Square Numbers, 9s,* and *The Last Six Facts*	DPP Item 8U is an inventory test on all five groups of multiplication facts. The *Multiplication Facts I Know* chart is updated.
Division Practice for the 5s and 10s	21–22	Unit 9: Items 9B, 9C, 9E, 9K, 9M, 9O, 9R, 9U & 9V	Unit 9 Parts 1 & 2	*Triangle Flash Cards: 5s* and *10s*	DPP Item 9U is a quiz on the division facts for the 5s and 10s. The *Division Facts I Know* chart is updated.
Division Practice for the 2s and 3s	23–24	Unit 10: Items 10B–10D, 10G, 10K, 10M, 10Q, 10W & 10X	Unit 10 Part 1	*Triangle Flash Cards: 2s* and *3s*	DPP Item 10W is a quiz on the division facts for the 2s and 3s. The *Division Facts I Know* chart is updated.
Division Practice for the Square Numbers	25–26	Unit 11: Items 11A, 11C, 11E, 11G, 11I, 11Q, 11T & 11U	Unit 11 Parts 1 & 3	*Triangle Flash Cards: Square Numbers*	DPP Item 11U is a quiz on the division facts for the Square Numbers. The *Division Facts I Know* chart is updated.
Division Practice for the 9s	27–29	Unit 12: Items 12B, 12C, 12G, 12H, 12K–12M, 12P & 12W	Unit 12 Part 1	*Triangle Flash Cards: 9s*	DPP Item 12W is a quiz on the division facts for the 9s. The *Division Facts I Know* chart is updated.

Grade 4 Math Facts Calendar *(continued)*

Math Facts Groups	Weeks	Daily Practice and Problems	Home Practice	Triangle Flash Cards	Facts Quizzes and Tests
Division Practice for The Last Six Facts	30–32	Unit 13: Items 13B–13D, 13H, 13K, 13Q, 13S & 13U	Unit 13 Part 1	*Triangle Flash Cards: The Last Six Facts*	DPP Item 13S is a quiz on the division facts for The Last Six Facts. The *Division Facts I Know* chart is updated.
Division Review for the 2s, 5s, 10s, and the Square Numbers	33	Unit 14: Items 14A–14C, 14G, 14K, 14M & 14O	Unit 14 Part 1	*Triangle Flash Cards: 2s, 5s, 10s,* and the *Square Numbers*	DPP Items 14M and 14O are quizzes on the division facts for the 2s, 5s, 10s, and the Square Numbers. The *Division Facts I Know* chart is updated.
Division Review for the 3s, 9s, and The Last Six Facts	34	Unit 15: Items 15B, 15E, 15G, 15J, 15L, 15M & 15O	Unit 15 Parts 1 & 2	*Triangle Flash Cards: 3s, 9s,* and *The Last Six Facts*	DPP Items 15M and 15O are quizzes on the division facts for the 3s, 9s, and The Last Six Facts. The *Division Facts I Know* chart is updated.
Division Review and Assessment for All Fact Groups	35–36	Unit 16: Items 16B, 16C, 16I, 16O, 16P & 16R	Unit 16 Parts 1 & 2	*Triangle Flash Cards: 5s, 10s, 2s, 3s, Square Numbers, 9s,* and *The Last Six Facts*	DPP Item 16R is an inventory test on all five groups of division facts. The *Division Facts I Know* chart is updated.

Section 5

Facts Distribution
Addition and Subtraction:
Review · Weeks 1-6

Weeks 1-6

Math Facts Groups	Weeks	Daily Practice and Problems	Home Practice	Triangle Flash Cards	Facts Quizzes and Tests
Addition and Subtraction Review	1–6	Unit 1: Items 1A–1E, 1K & 1M Unit 2: Items 2G–2I, 2M, 2O, 2Q, 2S & 2AA	Unit 1 Part 1 Unit 2 Parts 1 & 4		DPP Items 1K and 1M can serve as addition facts inventory tests. DPP Items 2M, 2O, 2Q, and 2S can serve as subtraction facts inventory tests.

Students may solve the items individually, in groups, or as a class. The items may also be assigned for homework.

Student Questions	Teacher Notes

1A Triangle Sums 1

What do you notice about the numbers in this triangle?

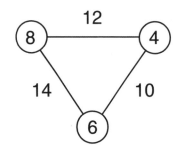

Find the missing numbers in these triangles.

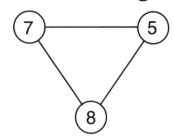

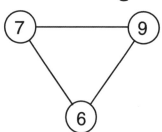

TIMS Bit

Students should see that the numbers in the circles, when added together, result in the number on the line that connects them. These puzzles require both logical thinking and knowledge of addition and subtraction facts.

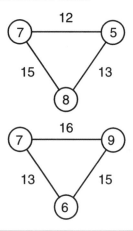

1B Addition Practice

1. 20 + 30 + 10 =

2. 40 + 10 + 20 =

3. 50 + 40 + 20 =

4. 60 + 60 + 10 =

5. 70 + 60 + 20 =

TIMS Task

Encourage students to share their strategies. Some students might use paper and pencil to solve the problems while other students solve them in their heads using skip counting and other counting strategies.

1. 60

2. 70

3. 110

4. 130

5. 150

1C Triangle Sums 2

Find the missing numbers in these triangles.

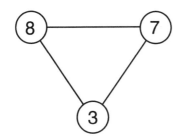 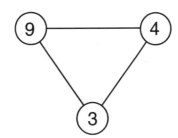

TIMS Bit

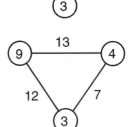

1D More Addition Practice

1. $70 + 40 =$

2. $60 + 50 + 20 =$

3. $80 + 50 =$

4. $60 + 90 =$

5. $130 + 90 =$

TIMS Task

Encourage students to share their strategies. Some students might use paper and pencil to solve the problems while other students solve them in their heads using strategies such as *using a ten, making a ten,* or *reasoning from known facts.* For descriptions of these addition fact strategies, see the TIMS Tutor: *Math Facts* in the *Teacher Implementation Guide.*

1. 110

2. 130

3. 130

4. 150

5. 220

1E Triangle Sums 3

Notice that numbers in the circles are missing in each of the triangle problems below. Find the missing numbers.

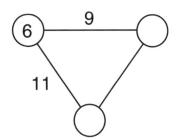

TIMS Bit

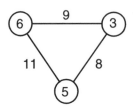

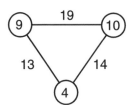

 1K Addition Test: *Doubles, 2s, 3s*

Take the diagnostic test *Doubles, 2s, 3s.* Your teacher will suggest some additional activities if you need more practice.

TIMS Bit

This diagnostic test, located on the following page, will allow you to identify students who need extra practice on the addition facts that can be solved using the strategies *using doubles* and *counting on*. For a description of these strategies, see the TIMS Tutor: *Math Facts* in the *Teacher Implementation Guide.*

We recommend 1 minute for this test. Allow students to change pens after the time is up and complete the remaining problems in a different color.

Students who need more practice can complete some of the activities provided in the Addition and Subtraction Math Facts Review section in the *Grade 4 Facts Resource Guide.* The games, *Add 1, 2, 3* and *Path to Glory*, provide practice with adding 1, 2, and 3.

Doubles, 2s, 3s

3 + 3 = _____   3 + 6 = _____

5 + 5 = _____   3 + 8 = _____

3 + 5 = _____   9 + 9 = _____

6 + 2 = _____   2 + 4 = _____

3 + 7 = _____   6 + 6 = _____

4 + 4 = _____   3 + 4 = _____

2 + 7 = _____   7 + 7 = _____

8 + 2 = _____   8 + 8 = _____

Addition Test: *More Addition Facts*

Take the diagnostic test *More Addition Facts.* Your teacher will suggest some additional activities if you need more practice.

TIMS Bit

This diagnostic test, located on the following page, will allow you to identify students who need extra practice on the "harder" addition facts: 4s, 5s, 6s, 7s, 8s, and 9s. The answers to these facts can be found using strategies such as *using a ten, making a ten,* and *using known facts.* For descriptions of these addition fact strategies, see the TIMS Tutor: *Math Facts* in the *Teacher Implementation Guide.*

We recommend 1 minute for this test. You may want to allow students to change pens after the time is up and complete the remaining problems in a different color.

Students who need more practice can complete some of the activities provided in the Addition and Subtraction Math Facts Review section in the *Grade 4 Facts Resource Guide.* Some appropriate activities are: *Add 4, 5, 6, Addition War, Triangle Flash Cards, Mixed-Up Addition Tables,* and *Line Math.*

More Addition Facts

5 + 4 = _____   9 + 5 = _____

6 + 7 = _____   4 + 6 = _____

4 + 7 = _____   6 + 8 = _____

8 + 4 = _____   9 + 4 = _____

9 + 6 = _____   7 + 8 = _____

7 + 9 = _____   5 + 6 = _____

5 + 7 = _____   8 + 9 = _____

8 + 5 = _____   9 + 3 = _____

10 + 4 = _____   10 + 9 = _____

Unit 1: Home Practice

Part 1 Practice

Solve the following addition problems. Try to solve the problems without paper and pencil. Be prepared to share your solution strategies.

1. $8 + 3 + 5 =$ _____

2. $9 + 7 + 5 =$ _____

3. $6 + 8 + 6 =$ _____

4. $4 + 8 + 9 =$ _____

5. $70 + 30 =$ _____

6. $60 + 20 + 30 =$ _____

7. $50 + 70 =$ _____

8. $30 + 50 + 70 =$ _____

9. $20 + 85 =$ _____

10. $10 + 80 + 15 =$ _____

Students may solve the items individually, in groups, or as a class. The items may also be assigned for homework.

Student Questions	Teacher Notes

2G Subtraction Practice

1. $92 - 3 =$ 2. $92 - 87 =$

3. $71 - 2 =$ 4. $43 - 4 =$

5. $41 - 39 =$ 6. $72 - 67 =$

TIMS Bit

Ask students to share their strategies. Some students may use strategies such as *counting up* or *counting back* to find the answers to these math facts. For descriptions of these subtraction fact strategies, see the TIMS Tutor: *Math Facts* in the *Teacher Implementation Guide.*

1. 89   2. 5

3. 69   4. 39

5. 2   6. 5

2H Magic Square

Put the digits 1, 2, 3, and 4 in the boxes below so that the sum of every row and every column is 10. Use four 1s, four 2s, four 3s, and four 4s.

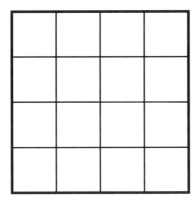

Hint: Instead of erasing, write four 1s, four 2s, four 3s, and four 4s on little slips of paper and move them around in the boxes until you find a solution.

TIMS Task

One of the possible solutions:

1	2	3	4
2	3	4	1
3	4	1	2
4	1	2	3

Note: The square does not fit the classic definition of a magic square, but it is similar. See DPP item F.

2I **Extra Subtraction Practice**

1. 120 − 90 =   2. 120 − 70 =

3. 160 − 80 =   4. 150 − 70 =

5. 170 − 80 =   6. 180 − 90 =

TIMS Bit N

Encourage students to share their strategies. Some students may use strategies, such as *using doubles, making a ten* (hundred), or *using a ten* (hundred). The addition doubles, e.g., 80 + 80 = 160 and 60 + 60 = 120, can be used to learn the subtraction "half-doubles" as well: 160 − 80 = 80 and 120 − 60 = 60. These facts can then be used to figure out close facts, such as 130 − 60 = 70 and 150 − 70 = 80.

Knowing the addition facts which have a sum of 100 can be helpful to solve a problem like 130 − 60 = 70 as well. To solve 130 − 60, a student might count up and make a hundred— 60 + 40 = 100; then 100 + 30 = 130. Thus 40 + 30 or 70 is the answer.

1. 30   2. 50

3. 80   4. 80

5. 90   6. 90

2M Subtraction Facts Test: Count-Ups

Take the subtraction diagnostic test *Subtraction Facts: Count-Ups.* Your teacher will suggest some additional activities if you need more practice.

TIMS Bit

This diagnostic test, located on the following page, will allow you to identify students who need extra practice on the subtraction facts that can be solved by using the strategy *counting up*. For a description of this strategy, see the TIMS Tutor: *Math Facts* in the *Teacher Implementation Guide.*

We recommend 1 minute for this test. Allow students to change pens after the time is up and complete the remaining problems in a different color.

For students who need more practice with these subtraction facts, see the Addition and Subtraction Math Facts Review in the *Grade 4 Facts Resource Guide.*

Subtraction Facts:
Count-Ups

$7 - 5 =$ _____ $8 - 5 =$ _____

$7 - 4 =$ _____ $9 - 7 =$ _____

$8 - 6 =$ _____ $6 - 3 =$ _____

$6 - 4 =$ _____ $9 - 6 =$ _____

$5 - 3 =$ _____ $10 - 8 =$ _____

$9 - 5 =$ _____ $11 - 8 =$ _____

$10 - 7 =$ _____ $8 - 7 =$ _____

$6 - 5 =$ _____ $7 - 6 =$ _____

Subtraction Facts Test: Count-Backs

Take the subtraction diagnostic test *Subtraction Facts: Count-Backs.* Your teacher will suggest some additional activities if you need more practice.

TIMS Bit

This diagnostic test, located on the following page, will allow you to identify students who need extra practice on the subtraction facts that can be solved by using the strategy *counting back*. For a description of this strategy, see the TIMS Tutor: *Math Facts* in the *Teacher Implementation Guide.*

We recommend 1 minute for this test. Allow students to change pens after the time is up and complete the remaining problems in a different color.

For students who need more practice with these subtraction facts, see the Addition and Subtraction Math Facts Review in the *Grade 4 Facts Resource Guide.*

Subtraction Facts: Count-Backs

7 − 2 = _____   4 − 3 = _____

10 − 3 = _____   4 − 2 = _____

9 − 3 = _____   10 − 2 = _____

9 − 1 = _____   9 − 2 = _____

5 − 0 = _____   8 − 3 = _____

5 − 2 = _____   8 − 2 = _____

11 − 2 = _____   11 − 3 = _____

6 − 2 = _____   8 − 1 = _____

Subtraction Facts Test: Using a Ten

Take the diagnostic test *Subtraction Facts: Using a Ten.* Your teacher will suggest some additional activities if you need more practice.

TIMS Bit

This diagnostic test, located on the following page, will allow you to identify students who need extra practice on the subtraction facts that can be solved by using the strategy *using a ten.* Since $14 - 9$ will be one more than $14 - 10$, students may reason that the answer will be 5, or $4 + 1$. For more information on subtraction facts strategies, see the TIMS Tutor: *Math Facts* in the *Teacher Implementation Guide.*

We recommend 1 minute for this test. Allow students to change pens after the time is up and complete the remaining problems in a different color.

For students who need more practice with these subtraction facts, see the Addition and Subtraction Math Facts Review in the *Grade 4 Facts Resource Guide.*

Subtraction Facts:
Using a Ten

14 – 9 = _____   17 – 8 = _____

16 – 9 = _____   16 – 6 = _____

15 – 9 = _____   18 – 8 = _____

14 – 4 = _____   13 – 8 = _____

17 – 9 = _____   13 – 7 = _____

15 – 10 = _____   15 – 7 = _____

17 – 10 = _____   16 – 7 = _____

13 – 9 = _____   11 – 9 = _____

14 – 8 = _____   12 – 2 = _____

2S Subtraction Facts Test: Doubles and Others

Take the diagnostic test *Subtraction Facts: Doubles and Others.* Your teacher will suggest some additional activities if you need more practice.

TIMS Bit

The test, located on the following page, will allow you to identify students who need extra practice on the subtraction facts that can be solved by using the strategy *using doubles* or other strategies, such as *making a ten.* The addition doubles, e.g., $8 + 8 = 16$, can be used to learn the subtraction "half-doubles" as well: $16 - 8 = 8$. The doubles can then be used to figure out related facts, such as $15 - 8 = 7$. For more information on subtraction facts strategies, see the TIMS Tutor: *Math Facts* in the *Teacher Implementation Guide.*

We recommend 1 minute for this test. Allow students to change pens after the time is up and complete the remaining problems in a different color.

For students who need more practice on these subtraction facts, see the Addition and Subtraction Math Facts Review in the *Grade 4 Facts Resource Guide.*

Subtraction Facts:
Doubles and Others

13 – 5 = _____   10 – 4 = _____

12 – 4 = _____   12 – 6 = _____

18 – 9 = _____   15 – 8 = _____

12 – 5 = _____   11 – 5 = _____

15 – 6 = _____   13 – 6 = _____

14 – 7 = _____   10 – 5 = _____

11 – 4 = _____   16 – 8 = _____

9 – 4 = _____   11 – 6 = _____

2AA More Subtraction Practice Again

1. 90 − 50 =

2. 110 − 40 =

3. 130 − 50 =

4. 100 − 30 =

5. 140 − 60 =

6. 160 − 70 =

TIMS Bit

Encourage students to share their strategies. For descriptions of subtraction fact strategies, see the TIMS Tutor: *Math Facts* in the *Teacher Implementation Guide.*

1. 40	2. 70
3. 80	4. 70
5. 80	6. 90

Unit 2: Home Practice

Part 1 Practice

1. 60 + 30 = _____
2. 90 + 30 = _____
3. 60 + 60 + 60 = _____
4. 80 − 60 = _____
5. 100 − 70 = _____
6. 130 − 60 = _____
7. 150 − 80 = _____
8. 150 − 90 = _____
9. 180 + 30 = _____
10. 210 − 20 = _____

Part 4 Subtraction Practice

Do the following problems in your head.

1. 11 − 9 = _____
2. 13 − 4 = _____
3. 12 − 3 = _____
4. 13 − 8 = _____
5. 12 − 8 = _____
6. 101 − 3 = _____
7. 92 − 4 = _____
8. 42 − 39 = _____
9. 171 − 167 = _____
10. 134 − 5 = _____

Facts Distribution
Multiplication and Division:
5s and 10s · Weeks 7-8

Math Facts Groups	Weeks	Daily Practice and Problems	Home Practice	Triangle Flash Cards	Facts Quizzes and Tests
Multiplication Review and Division Practice for the 5s and 10s	7–8	The lesson, *Multiplying and Dividing with 5s and 10s* (Unit 3 Lesson 1), begins the formal Grade 4 math facts program. Complete that lesson prior to beginning the DPP items listed below. Unit 3: Items 3B, 3C, 3E, 3F, 3H & 3K–3M	Unit 3 Parts 1, 4 & 5	*Triangle Flash Cards: 5s and 10s*	DPP Item 3M is a quiz on the multiplication facts for the 5s and 10s. The *Multiplication Facts I Know* chart is updated.

LESSON GUIDE

Multiplying and Dividing with 5s and 10s

Estimated Class Sessions: **2**

This lesson introduces the yearlong review of the multiplication facts and launches the systematic strategies-based approach to learning the division facts. Students solve word problems to develop and enhance their understanding of the division operation. Fact families are introduced so students can use multiplication facts to learn related division facts. They use flash cards to assess their fluency with multiplication facts for the fives and tens. They study multiplication with zero and one.

Key Content

* Self-assessing the multiplication and division facts for the 5s and 10s.
* Using known multiplication facts to learn related division facts.
* Multiplying by 0 and 1.
* Writing the four related number sentences in a fact family.

Key Vocabulary

dividend
division sentence
divisor
fact family
factors
product
quotient
turn-around facts

Curriculum Sequence

Before This Unit

In third grade, students studied all the multiplication facts. They explored division concepts in Grade 3 Units 7, 11, and 19. Students explored multiplication by zero and one in the Adventure Book story *Cipher Force* in Grade 3 Unit 11 Lesson 7.

After This Unit

Students continue reviewing the multiplication facts and develop strategies for the division facts in Units 4–8. In Units 9–16, they develop fluency with the division facts while maintaining their fluency with the multiplication facts.

Materials List

Print Materials for Students

		Math Facts and Daily Practice and Problems	Activity	Homework
Student Books	**Student Guide**		*Multiplying and Dividing with 5s and 10s* Pages 58–62	*Multiplying and Dividing with 5s and 10s* Homework Section Page 63
	Discovery Assignment Book		*Triangle Flash Cards: 5s* Page 29, *Triangle Flash Cards: 10s* Page 31, and *Multiplication Facts I Know,* Page 33	Home Practice Parts 1 & 4 Pages 23 & 25
Teacher Resources	**Facts Resource Guide** ⊙	DPP Items 3B & 3C Use *Triangle Flash Cards: 5s* and *Triangle Flash Cards: 10s* to review the multiplication facts for the 5s and 10s		
	Unit Resource Guide	DPP Items A–D Pages 13–14 *Information for Parents: Grade 4 Math Facts Philosophy* Page 8 ⊙		
	Generic Section ⊙			*Triangle Flash Cards: 5s* and *Triangle Flash Cards: 10s,* 1 each per student (optional)

⊙ *available on Teacher Resource CD*

All Transparency Masters, Blackline Masters, and Assessment Blackline Masters in the Unit Resource Guide are on the Teacher Resource CD.

Supplies for Each Student

1 or 2 envelopes for storing flash cards

Materials for the Teacher

Transparencies of *Triangle Flash Cards: 5s* and *Triangle Flash Cards: 10s* (Discovery Assignment Book) Pages 29 and 31

Content Note

In Units 3–7, students use the *Triangle Flash Cards* and the *Facts I Know* charts only with the multiplication facts. They will build strategies for the division facts in Units 3–8 and use the *Triangle Flash Cards* to develop fluency with the division facts in Units 8–16. Reviewing the multiplication facts will facilitate their work with the division facts. Students will use the same groups of flash cards to study the division facts in Units 9–16.

 Multiplying and Dividing with 5s and 10s

Using Fact Families – Multiplying and Dividing with 5s and 10s

Jackson's Hardware Store decided to donate 30 basketballs to the schools in the neighborhood.

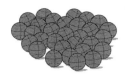

John and his father went to pick up the basketballs for Bessie Coleman school. When they arrived at the store there were people from four other schools waiting to pick up their basketballs. John helped divide the thirty basketballs into five groups.

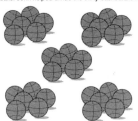

Each of the 5 schools got 6 new basketballs.

The **division sentence** for this is 30 ÷ 5 = 6. The answer to a division problem is called the **quotient**. In this sentence the quotient is six. Thirty, or the number to be divided, is the **dividend**. The **divisor** is five.

58   SG · Grade 4 · Unit 3 · Lesson 1   Multiplying and Dividing with 5s and 10s

Student Guide - Page 58

Before the Activity

Part 3 of this lesson introduces students to *Triangle Flash Cards*. The *Triangle Flash Cards* for the 5s and 10s are located in the *Discovery Assignment Book*. Have students cut out the cards from their books and place them in envelopes.

Developing the Activity

Part 1. Using Fact Families: Multiplying and Dividing with 5s and 10s

The vignette on the first page of the *Multiplying and Dividing with 5s and 10s* Activity Pages in the *Student Guide* presents a situation that illustrates the relationship between two facts ($30 \div 5 = 6$ and $5 \times 6 = 30$). It introduces students to the use of **fact families.** Students should see that division is the opposite (inverse) operation of multiplication.

Multiplication can be thought of as repeated addition, for example, adding five groups of six for a total of 30 basketballs. Division can be thought of as repeated subtraction, for example, subtracting five groups of six basketballs from 30.

Discuss *Question 1* in the *Student Guide*. Ask:

- *What information is given in the problem?* (The total number of soccer balls, 30, and the number of balls in each group, 6.)

- *What does the answer, the* **quotient,** *tell you?* (The number of schools that will receive soccer balls.)

- *How is* **Question 1** *different from the basketball story? Think about what the problem tells you and what you need to find out.* (In the story we know the number of schools, 5, and we want to find out the number of basketballs for each school, 6. In *Question 1* we know the number of soccer balls each school will receive, 6, and we want to know how many schools will receive them, 5.)

- *What number sentence represents the basketball story?* ($30 \div 5 = 6$)

- *What is a number sentence for the soccer ball problem?* ($30 \div 6 = 5$)

- *How are they alike?* (They have the same numbers. Thirty is the **dividend** in both sentences.)

- *How are they different?* (The **divisors** and quotients change. Thirty basketballs are divided into five groups in the basketball story. Thirty soccer balls are divided into groups of six in the soccer ball problem.)

- *How can we check a division problem? Give me an example.* (Multiply the quotient by the divisor. To check 30 ÷ 6 = 5, multiply 5 times 6 to get 30.)
- *What can we say about multiplication and division together?* (They are opposites. They "undo" each other.)

Write all four number sentences on the board or the overhead projector. Tell students that the four related sentences make a **fact family.**

$$5 \times 6 = 30 \qquad 6 \times 5 = 30$$
$$30 \div 5 = 6 \qquad 30 \div 6 = 5$$

Remind students that the two multiplication sentences are **turn-around facts** (5×6 and 6×5). Students should remember turn-around facts from third grade.

Ask students to work through *Questions 2–5* in pairs. *Questions 2–4* provide different division situations. Having students draw pictures reinforces their understanding of the concept represented by the number sentences. For *Question 5,* students should understand that knowing one member of a fact family helps them learn the other members of the same fact family.

Questions 6–15 provide practice with fact families. They require students to use math facts in the context of money and other contexts. These questions can also be assigned for homework.

Journal Prompt

Why do you think we call four facts like these ($5 \times 6 = 30, 6 \times 5 = 30, 30 \div 5 = 6, 30 \div 6 = 5$) a fact family?

Content Note

Division can be applied to two types of situations. The first is called partitive (sharing) division and is applied to problems like the basketball giveaway story. The total number of objects and the desired number of groups (partitions) are known. What is not known and what will be determined by the answer is the number of objects in each group. Thirty basketballs shared among five schools results in six basketballs per school.

The second type of division situation is known as measurement (subtractive) division. It is illustrated by *Question 1* in the *Student Guide*. In this case, the total number of objects to be distributed and the size (or measure) of the groups are known. What is not known and what will be determined by the answer is the number of groups that will result. Thirty soccer balls divided into groups of six balls each results in five groups.

The labels for these two situations are not important here. However, it is important for students to have opportunities to solve both types of problems.

Then John told everyone that he would label all the basketballs with the correct school name. Everyone brought the new basketballs back to him for labeling, one school at a time. John added 6 + 6 + 6 + 6 + 6. He knew this was the same as five groups of six or 5 times 6, or 30 basketballs in all.

John knew that 5 × 6 = 30 is related to the division sentence 30 ÷ 5 = 6. There are two more sentences that are related: 6 × 5 = 30 and 30 ÷ 6 = 5. We call all four of these sentences together a **fact family.**

1. Jackson's Hardware also gave away a total of 30 soccer balls. Each school received a crate of six balls.
   A. How many schools got soccer balls? Write a number sentence to describe this.
   B. What does each number in the sentence represent?

2. John found he had 30 marbles at home and decided to give an equal number of marbles to each of his three sisters. How many marbles did John give to each sister? Draw a picture for this problem and describe it using a division sentence. Write another number sentence that is in the same fact family.

3. Nila wrote a division story for 20 ÷ 5. Nila drew a picture for her story.

   A. What is another number sentence that is in the same fact family as 20 ÷ 5?
   B. Write a division story for 50 ÷ 10. Draw a picture for your story and write a number sentence. Write three more sentences that are in the same fact family.

Student Guide - Page 59

---

4. Maya baked chocolate chip cookies. She counted out 45 cookies and put an equal number in each of 9 bags. Then she gave one bag of cookies to 9 friends.
   A. How many cookies did she give each friend? Write a number sentence for this story.
   B. Write a multiplication number sentence in the same fact family. What do the numbers in the multiplication sentence represent?

5. Which of the following number sentences is in the same fact family as 5 × 8 = 40?
   a) 40 ÷ 10 = 4   b) 40 ÷ 5 = 8   c) 8 × 4 = 32   d) 8 × 5 = 40

Solve Questions 6–15. Use fact families, manipulatives, or other strategies. Write a number sentence for each problem. Then write the other three sentences in the same fact family.

6. How many dimes are in 80 cents?
7. How many nickels are in 35 cents?
8. How many nickels are in 15 cents?
9. How many nickels are in 40 cents?
10. How many dimes are in 60 cents?
11. How many nickels are in 20 cents?
12. How many dimes are in 40 cents?
13. Maya gets paid for helping her neighbor with her baby one afternoon each week. She saves all the money she gets and after five weeks, she has $25. How much money does Maya get paid each week? Write a number sentence.
14. How many weeks will Maya have to help her neighbor to make $45? Write a number sentence.
15. John lives 4 blocks from school. It takes him 20 minutes to walk to school. If John walks steadily, how long does it take John to walk one block? Write a number sentence.

Student Guide - Page 60

Multiplying with 0 and 1

16. Think about multiplication as repeated addition of groups. Three groups of five makes fifteen. $3 \times 5 = 15$. Now think about what happens when you multiply with 1 or 0. How many groups do you have? How many are in each group? Try the following problems. You may want to use your calculator.

A. $5 \times 0 =$ B. $5 \times 1 =$

C. $10 \times 0 =$ D. $1 \times 10 =$

E. $0 \times 98 =$ F. $98 \times 1 =$

G. $0 \times 5348 =$ H. $1 \times 5348 =$

17. A. What can you say about multiplying numbers by 0? Explain.
   B. What can you say about multiplying numbers by 1? Explain.

Multiplication Facts and *Triangle Flash Cards*

With a partner, use the directions below and your *Triangle Flash Cards: 5s* and *Triangle Flash Cards: 10s* to practice the multiplication facts.

- One partner covers the shaded number, the largest number on the card. This number will be the answer to the multiplication problem. It is called the **product.**

$5 \times 4 = ?$

$4 \times 5 = ?$

- The second person multiplies the two uncovered numbers (one in a circle, one in a square). These are the two **factors.** It does not matter which of the factors is said first. 4×5 and 5×4 both equal 20. $4 \times 5 = 20$ and $5 \times 4 = 20$ are called **turn-around facts.**

Multiplying and Dividing with 5s and 10s   SG · Grade 4 · Unit 3 · Lesson 1   61

Student Guide - Page 61

- Separate the facts into three piles: those facts you know and can answer quickly, those that you can figure out with a strategy, and those that you need to learn.
- Discuss how you can figure out facts that you do not recall right away. Share your strategies with your partner.
- Practice the last two piles again and then make a list of the facts you need to practice at home for homework.
- Circle the facts you know quickly on your *Multiplication Facts I Know* chart. Remember that if you know one fact, you also know its turn-around fact. Circle both on your chart.
- Review your answers to Question 17.
- You will continue to use *Triangle Flash Cards* to study other groups of facts. If you know one or two of the multiplication facts in a fact family, you can use those facts to help you learn the division facts.

Multiplication Facts I Know

×	0	1	2	3	4	5	6	7	8	9	10
0	0	0	0	0	0	0	0	0	0	0	0
1	0	1	2	3	4	5	6	7	8	9	10
2	0	2	4	6	8	10	12	14	16	18	20
3	0	3	6	9	12	15	18	21	24	27	30
4	0	4	8	12	16	20	24	28	32	36	40
5	0	5	10	15	20	25	30	35	40	45	50
6	0	6	12	18	24	30	36	42	48	54	60
7	0	7	14	21	28	35	42	49	56	63	70
8	0	8	16	24	32	40	48	56	64	72	80
9	0	9	18	27	36	45	54	63	72	81	90
10	0	10	20	30	40	50	60	70	80	90	100

62   SG · Grade 4 · Unit 3 · Lesson 1   Multiplying and Dividing with 5s and 10s

Student Guide - Page 62

Part 2. Multiplying with 0 and 1

Have students complete *Questions 16–17* in pairs before discussing them together as a class. Continue the discussion:

- *How can both 5 × 0 and 10 × 0 equal the same answer?* (Possible response: Five groups of zero objects and ten groups of zero objects are both zero.)

- *Make up a number story about* **Question 16D.** (One possible story: Jackson's Hardware Store gave away one box of ten Ping-Pong balls. How many balls did the store give away?)

- *What is one times ten million? How do you know?* (ten million. One group of ten million is just ten million.)

- *What is the product of one and any number? How do you know?* (that number. Because one group of any number is that number.)

- *What is zero times ten million? How do you know?* (zero. If I have zero groups of ten million, I have zero.)

- *What is the product of any number and zero? How do you know?* (zero. Repeated addition of zero any number of times is zero and zero groups of any number is still zero.)

Part 3. Multiplication Facts and Triangle Flash Cards

The *Student Guide* outlines how students use the *Triangle Flash Cards* for multiplication, and Part 1 of the Home Practice in the *Discovery Assignment Book* provides a quick review. Partners cover the number that is shaded (the largest number on the card). This is the **product,** the answer to the multiplication problem that the other two numbers (the **factors**) present. The student who is being quizzed multiplies the two numbers that are showing, gives the answer, and the answer is checked.

As their partners quiz them on the facts, students sort the cards into three piles—those facts they know and can answer quickly, those facts they know using a strategy, and those facts they need to learn. Then each student begins his or her *Multiplication Facts I Know* chart found in the *Discovery Assignment Book.* Students circle only those facts that they know and can answer quickly. However, remind students that if they know a fact, they also know its turn-around fact. So, if they circle $5 \times 3 = 15$, they can also circle $3 \times 5 = 15$. Also remind students of the discussion of multiplication by zero and one. Using what they learned from *Questions 16* and *17,* they can circle the facts for zero and one. Students make a list of the facts for the fives and tens that they did not circle on their charts. They take this list home along with their flash cards so that they can practice the facts they need to study with a family member.

Students will work with the *Triangle Flash Cards* for the division facts in Units 9–16 and record their progress on a *Division Facts I Know* chart at that time. Until then, they use flash cards and the chart primarily for multiplication facts. At the same time, students are practicing division facts in activities, labs, and the Daily Practice and Problems. As students review the multiplication facts through practice with fact families, they will see their fluency with the division facts increase.

DPP items B, C, E, F, H, K, and L provide further practice with the multiplication and division facts for the fives and tens. A quiz on the multiplication facts for the fives and tens is provided in Bit M. Inform students when the quiz will be given so they can practice at home. As students encounter multiplication problems with the facts, encourage them to share their strategies. The fives and tens are easily solved using skip counting. For descriptions of other multiplication facts strategies, see the TIMS Tutor: *Math Facts* in the *Teacher Implementation Guide*.

Content Note

This lesson illustrates the following mathematical properties:

Identity Property of Multiplication. This is also known as the Property of One for Multiplication. One times any number is that number. Using variables, $n \times 1 = n$.

Zero Property of Multiplication. Any number times zero is zero. Using variables, $n \times 0 = 0$.

Commutative Property of Multiplication. This is also known as the Order Property of Multiplication. Changing the order of the factors does not change the product. For example, $3 \times 5 = 5 \times 3 = 15$. Using variables, $n \times m = m \times n$.

It is not necessary at this point that students know the names of these properties or be able to state them using variables. It is sufficient that they can use the ideas when they solve problems.

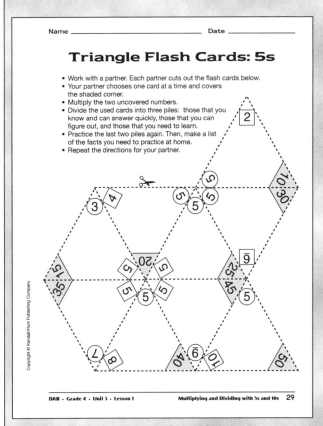

Discovery Assignment Book - Page 29

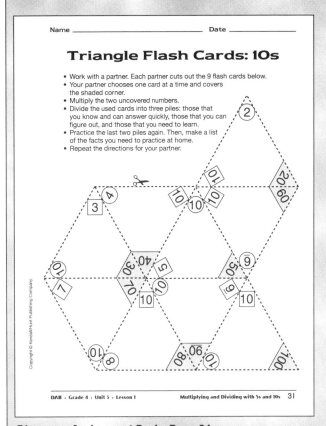

Discovery Assignment Book - Page 31

Daily Practice and Problems:
Task and Challenge for Lesson 1

B. Task: Nickels (URG p. 13)

What is the value of:

1. 5 nickels?
2. 8 nickels?
3. 6 dimes?
4. 2 dimes and 6 nickels?

How many nickels in:

5. 15¢
6. 45¢
7. 20¢
8. 35¢

D. Challenge: What Are Words Worth? (URG p. 14)

Make yourself a chart where the letter A = 1¢, B = 2¢, C = 3¢, and so on until you get to Z = 26¢. You can now find the value of words by adding together the amounts for each letter in the word. For example, the word *cat* is worth 24¢ because C = 3¢, A = 1¢, and T = 20¢.

1. What is the value of the word *money*?

2. Which word is more valuable, *diamond or emerald*?

3. Try to find a word that is worth exactly $1.00.

4. Find the shortest word you can that is worth more than $1.00.

5. What is the most valuable word you can find?

Content Note

Because the math facts program is closely linked to the recommended schedule for teaching lessons, classrooms that differ significantly from the suggested pacing will need to make accommodations in order to ensure that students receive a consistent program of math facts practice and assessment throughout the year. The *Grade 4 Facts Resource Guide* outlines a schedule for math facts practice and assessment in classrooms that are moving much more slowly through lessons than is recommended in the lesson guides. The *Grade 4 Facts Resource Guide* contains all components of the math facts program, including DPP items, flash cards, *Facts I Know* charts, and assessments.

Suggestions for Teaching the Lesson

Math Facts

- In Task B, students use math facts to solve problems involving nickels and dimes. Bit C provides practice with fact families.

- Part 1 of the Home Practice reminds students to take home their flash cards for the fives and tens. Students may practice these facts with a family member. Also send home the *Information for Parents: Grade 4 Math Facts Philosophy.* This information sheet can be found immediately following the Background.

- Part 4 of the Home Practice provides additional practice with fact families.

Answers for Part 4 of the Home Practice can be found in the Answer Key at the end of this lesson and at the end of this unit.

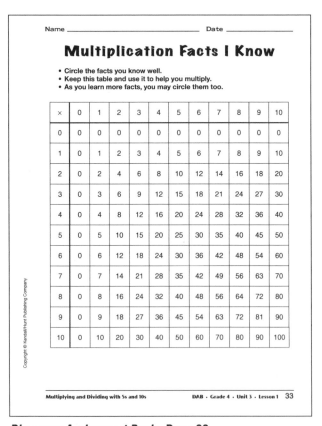

Discovery Assignment Book - Page 33

Homework and Practice

- Assign homework *Questions 1–10* in the *Student Guide.*

- DPP Bit A provides practice identifying acute, obtuse, and right triangles.

Extension

Item D challenges students to find the value of words if an A is worth 1¢, a B is worth 2¢, and so on. Students enjoy solving the problems while practicing addition and estimation.

Homework

Dear Family Member:

Your child is reviewing the multiplication facts and learning the division facts for fives and tens by studying fact families. For example, $5 \times 4 = 20$, $4 \times 5 = 20$, $20 \div 5 = 4$, $20 \div 4 = 5$ is a fact family. Once a student learns the multiplication facts, learning the division facts becomes easier. Using fact families is a good strategy for solving most of the problems below. Remind your child to bring home the flash cards for the fives and tens. Help him or her study these facts.

Thank you for your cooperation.

1. How many dimes in 90 cents?

2. How many nickels in 30 cents?

3. Banks wrap dimes into packs of 50 dimes. If Nila takes 70 dimes to the bank to be wrapped, how many packs will she get? How many dollars will this be? How many dimes will be left over?

4. There are 20 Little League teams in the city. The League places 10 teams in a division. How many divisions will there be in the city? Write a number sentence for this story and all the number sentences in this fact family.

5. Write a story to show $45 \div 9$. Draw a picture to go with your story and write a number sentence. Write all the other number sentences that are in this fact family.

6. Show two ways you can have 25 cents if you have only dimes and nickels.

7. Show three ways you can have 40 cents if you have only dimes and nickels.

8. Chewy Candies come in packs of five. Irma has 3 packs, Michael has 5 packs, Romesh has 1 pack, and Jessie has no packs.

   A. How many candies does each student have? Write a number sentence for each student.

   B. How many candies do they have altogether?

9. Jacob has 60 cents and needs $1.00 for a show. How many dimes does he need to make $1.00?

10. A pack of Chewy Candies costs 15 cents. How many packs can you buy with $1.00? Explain your solution.

Student Guide - Page 63

Name _____ Date _____

Unit 3: Home Practice

Part 1   *Triangle Flash Cards: 5s and 10s*
Study for the quiz on the multiplication facts for the fives and tens. Take home your *Triangle Flash Cards: 5s* and *10s* and your list of facts you need to study.

Here's how to use the flash cards. Ask a family member to choose one flash card at a time. He or she should cover the corner containing the highest number. This number will be the answer to a multiplication problem. Multiply the two uncovered numbers.

Study the math facts in small groups. Choose eight to ten facts to study each night. Your teacher will tell you when the quiz on the fives and tens will be.

Part 2   Addition and Subtraction
Use paper and pencil to solve the following problems.

1. 644	2. 76	3. 386	4. 196
+ 53	+ 29	− 21	− 77

5. 938	6. 4015	7. 5048	8. 4653
− 449	+ 488	− 274	+ 5664

Choose one problem. Be ready to explain how you can tell if the answer is reasonable.

Discovery Assignment Book - Page 23

Name _____ Date _____

Part 4   Fact Families
For each fact given, write the other three members of the same fact family.

A. $6 \times 5 = 30$ _____
           _____
           _____

B. $90 \div 10 = 9$ _____
           _____
           _____

C. $15 \div 5 = 3$ _____
           _____
           _____

D. $5 \times 9 = 45$ _____
           _____
           _____

E. $5 \times 10 = 50$ _____
           _____
           _____

Discovery Assignment Book - Page 25

AT A GLANCE

Math Facts and Daily Practice and Problems

DPP Bit A reviews angles. Items B and C provide practice with the multiplication and division facts for the fives and tens. Challenge D is a problem-solving activity.

Before the Activity

Students cut out the *Triangle Flash Cards: 5s* and *10s* from the *Discovery Assignment Book* and store them in envelopes.

Part 1. Using Fact Families: Multiplying and Dividing with 5s and 10s

1. Students are introduced to fact families and begin learning their division facts for the fives and tens.
2. Students discuss the relationship between multiplication and division *(Question 1)*.
3. Students work on *Questions 2–5* in pairs and then share their answers with the class.
4. Students practice with fact families *(Questions 6–15)*.

Part 2. Multiplying with 0 and 1

Students explore multiplication with 0 and 1 *(Questions 16–17)*.

Part 3. Multiplication Facts and *Triangle Flash Cards*

Students review the multiplication facts for the fives and tens by using *Triangle Flash Cards*.

Homework

1. Assign Parts 1 and 4 of the Home Practice.
2. Assign *Questions 1–10* in the Homework section of the *Student Guide*.

Assessment

Students begin a record of their progress with the facts by using the *Multiplication Facts I Know* chart in the *Discovery Assignment Book*.

Notes:

Student Guide

Questions 1–17 (SG pp. 59–61)

1.* **A.** 5 schools; $30 \div 6 = 5$

   B. 30 soccer balls, 6 balls in a crate, 5 schools

2.* 10 marbles; $30 \div 3 = 10$. Other sentences in the same fact family are $30 \div 10 = 3$, $3 \times 10 = 30, 10 \times 3 = 30$.

3.* **A.** Possible answers: $20 \div 4 = 5, 4 \times 5 = 20$, $5 \times 4 = 20$.

   B. Answers will vary.

4.* **A.** 5 cookies, $45 \div 9 = 5$

   B. $5 \times 9 = 45$ (or $9 \times 5 = 45$) 5 cookies in a bag, 9 bags (or 9 friends), 45 cookies in all

5. b and d are in the same fact family

6. 8 dimes, $80 \div 10 = 8, 80 \div 8 = 10$, $10 \times 8 = 80, 8 \times 10 = 80$

7. 7 nickels, $35 \div 5 = 7, 35 \div 7 = 5, 7 \times 5 = 35$, $5 \times 7 = 35$

8. 3 nickels, $15 \div 5 = 3, 15 \div 3 = 5, 3 \times 5 = 15$, $5 \times 3 = 15$

9. 8 nickels, $40 \div 5 = 8, 40 \div 8 = 5, 8 \times 5 = 40$, $5 \times 8 = 40$

10. 6 dimes, $60 \div 10 = 6, 60 \div 6 = 10$, $6 \times 10 = 60, 10 \times 6 = 60$

11. 4 nickels, $20 \div 5 = 4, 20 \div 4 = 5, 5 \times 4 = 20$, $4 \times 5 = 20$

12. 4 dimes, $40 \div 10 = 4, 40 \div 4 = 10$, $4 \times 10 = 40, 10 \times 4 = 40$

13. $25 \div 5 = 5$ dollars per week

14. $45 \div 5 = 9$ weeks

15. $20 \div 4 = 5$ minutes

16.* **A.** 0   **B.** 5

   C. 0   **D.** 10

   E. 0   **F.** 98

   G. 0   **H.** 5348

17.* **A.** Any number multiplied by 0 is 0. Zero groups of any number is zero.

   B. Any number multiplied by 1 is the number itself. One group of any number is that number.

Homework

Questions 1–10 (SG p. 63)

1. 9 dimes

2. 6 nickels

3. 1 pack of dimes, $5.00, and 20 dimes left over ($2.00).

4. 2 divisions in the city; $20 \div 10 = 2$. Other number sentences in the fact family are $20 \div 2 = 10, 2 \times 10 = 20, 10 \times 2 = 20$.

5. Answers will vary. The other number sentences in the same fact family are $45 \div 5 = 9$, $5 \times 9 = 45, 9 \times 5 = 45$.

6. Two dimes and one nickel, one dime and three nickels.

7. Three dimes and two nickels, two dimes and four nickels, one dime and six nickels.

8. **A.** Irma had 15 candies, Michael had 25 candies, Romesh had 5 candies, and Jessie had no candy. $3 \times 5 = 15, 5 \times 5 = 25$, $1 \times 5 = 5, 0 \times 5 = 0$.

   B. 45 candies

9. 4 dimes

10. 6 packs. Possible strategy: 2 packs cost 30¢. $30¢ \times 3 = 90¢$. So 6 packs cost 90¢.

Discovery Assignment Book

**Home Practice (DAB p. 25)

Part 4. Fact Families

Questions A–E

   A. $30 \div 5 = 6, 5 \times 6 = 30$, $30 \div 6 = 5$

   B. $9 \times 10 = 90, 10 \times 9 = 90$, $90 \div 9 = 10$

   C. $3 \times 5 = 15, 15 \div 3 = 5$, $5 \times 3 = 15$

   D. $9 \times 5 = 45, 45 \div 5 = 9$, $45 \div 9 = 5$

   E. $10 \times 5 = 50, 50 \div 5 = 10$, $50 \div 10 = 5$

*Answers and/or discussion are included in the Lesson Guide.

**Answers for all the Home Practice in the *Discovery Assignment Book* are at the end of the unit.

Using Fact Families – Multiplying and Dividing with 5s and 10s

Jackson's Hardware Store decided to donate 30 basketballs to the schools in the neighborhood.

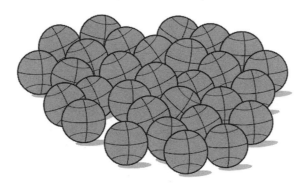

John and his father went to pick up the basketballs for Bessie Coleman school. When they arrived at the store there were people from four other schools waiting to pick up their basketballs. John helped divide the thirty basketballs into five groups.

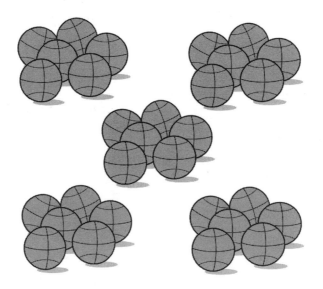

Each of the 5 schools got 6 new basketballs.

The **division sentence** for this is 30 ÷ 5 = 6. The answer to a division problem is called the **quotient.** In this sentence the quotient is six. Thirty, or the number to be divided, is the **dividend. The divisor** is five.

Then John told everyone that he would label all the basketballs with the correct school name. Everyone brought the new basketballs back to him for labeling, one school at a time. John added 6 + 6 + 6 + 6 + 6. He knew this was the same as five groups of six or 5 times 6, or 30 basketballs in all.

John knew that 5 × 6 = 30 is related to the division sentence 30 ÷ 5 = 6. There are two more sentences that are related: 6 × 5 = 30 and 30 ÷ 6 = 5. We call all four of these sentences together a **fact family.**

1. Jackson's Hardware also gave away a total of 30 soccer balls. Each school received a crate of six balls.

   A. How many schools got soccer balls? Write a number sentence to describe this.

   B. What does each number in the sentence represent?

2. John found he had 30 marbles at home and decided to give an equal number of marbles to each of his three sisters. How many marbles did John give to each sister? Draw a picture for this problem and describe it using a division sentence. Write another number sentence that is in the same fact family.

3. Nila wrote a division story for 20 ÷ 5. Nila drew a picture for her story.

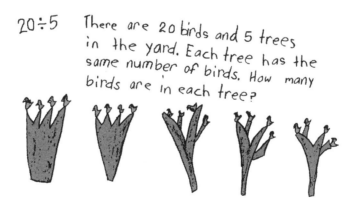

20 ÷ 5   There are 20 birds and 5 trees in the yard. Each tree has the same number of birds. How many birds are in each tree?

   A. What is another number sentence that is in the same fact family as 20 ÷ 5?

   B. Write a division story for 50 ÷ 10. Draw a picture for your story and write a number sentence. Write three more sentences that are in the same fact family.

4. Maya baked chocolate chip cookies. She counted out 45 cookies and put an equal number in each of 9 bags. Then she gave one bag of cookies to 9 friends.

   A. How many cookies did she give each friend? Write a number sentence for this story.

   B. Write a multiplication number sentence in the same fact family. What do the numbers in the multiplication sentence represent?

5. Which of the following number sentences is in the same fact family as $5 \times 8 = 40$?

   a) $40 \div 10 = 4$ b) $40 \div 5 = 8$ c) $8 \times 4 = 32$ d) $8 \times 5 = 40$

Solve Questions 6–15. Use fact families, manipulatives, or other strategies. Write a number sentence for each problem. Then write the other three sentences in the fact family.

6. How many dimes are in 80 cents?

7. How many nickels are in 35 cents?

8. How many nickels are in 15 cents?

9. How many nickels are in 40 cents?

10. How many dimes are in 60 cents?

11. How many nickels are in 20 cents?

12. How many dimes are in 40 cents?

13. Maya gets paid for helping her neighbor with her baby one afternoon each week. She saves all the money she gets and after five weeks, she has $25. How much money does Maya get paid each week? Write a number sentence.

14. How many weeks will Maya have to help her neighbor to make $45? Write a number sentence.

15. John lives 4 blocks from school. It takes him 20 minutes to walk to school. If John walks steadily, how long does it take John to walk one block? Write a number sentence.

Multiplying with 0 and 1

16. Think about multiplication as repeated addition of groups. Three groups of five makes fifteen. $3 \times 5 = 15$. Now think about what happens when you multiply with 1 or 0. How many groups do you have? How many are in each group? Try the following problems. You may want to use your calculator.

   A. $5 \times 0 =$

   B. $5 \times 1 =$

   C. $10 \times 0 =$

   D. $1 \times 10 =$

   E. $0 \times 98 =$

   F. $98 \times 1 =$

   G. $0 \times 5348 =$

   H. $1 \times 5348 =$

17. A. What can you say about multiplying numbers by 0? Explain.

   B. What can you say about multiplying numbers by 1? Explain.

Multiplication Facts and *Triangle Flash Cards*

With a partner, use the directions below and your *Triangle Flash Cards: 5s* and *Triangle Flash Cards: 10s* to practice the multiplication facts.

- One partner covers the shaded number, the largest number on the card. This number will be the answer to the multiplication problem. It is called the **product.**

- The second person multiplies the two uncovered numbers (one in a circle, one in a square). These are the two **factors.** It does not matter which of the factors is said first.
4×5 and 5×4 both equal 20.
$4 \times 5 = 20$ and $5 \times 4 = 20$ are called **turn-around facts.**

$5 \times 4 = ?$

$4 \times 5 = ?$

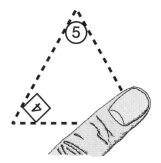

- Separate the facts into three piles: those facts you know and can answer quickly, those that you can figure out with a strategy, and those that you need to learn.

- Discuss how you can figure out facts that you do not recall right away. Share your strategies with your partner.

- Practice the last two piles again and then make a list of the facts you need to practice at home for homework.

- Circle the facts you know quickly on your *Multiplication Facts I Know* chart. Remember that if you know one fact, you also know its turn-around fact. Circle both on your chart.

- Review your answers to Question 17.

- You will continue to use *Triangle Flash Cards* to study other groups of facts. If you know one or two of the multiplication facts in a fact family, you can use those facts to help you learn the division facts.

Multiplication Facts I Know

×	0	1	2	3	4	5	6	7	8	9	10
0	0	0	0	0	0	0	0	0	0	0	0
1	0	1	2	3	4	5	6	7	8	9	10
2	0	2	4	6	8	10	12	14	16	18	20
3	0	3	6	9	12	15	18	21	24	27	30
4	0	4	8	12	16	(20)	24	28	32	36	40
5	0	5	10	15	(20)	25	30	35	40	45	50
6	0	6	12	18	24	30	36	42	48	54	60
7	0	7	14	21	28	35	42	49	56	63	70
8	0	8	16	24	32	40	48	56	64	72	80
9	0	9	18	27	36	45	54	63	72	81	90
10	0	10	20	30	40	50	60	70	80	90	100

Homework

Dear Family Member:

Your child is reviewing the multiplication facts and learning the division facts for fives and tens by studying fact families. For example, $5 \times 4 = 20$, $4 \times 5 = 20$, $20 \div 5 = 4$, $20 \div 4 = 5$ is a fact family. Once a student learns the multiplication facts, learning the division facts becomes easier. Using fact families is a good strategy for solving most of the problems below. Remind your child to bring home the flash cards for the fives and tens. Help him or her study these facts.

Thank you for your cooperation.

1. How many dimes in 90 cents?

2. How many nickels in 30 cents?

3. Banks wrap dimes into packs of 50 dimes. If Nila takes 70 dimes to the bank to be wrapped, how many packs will she get? How many dollars will this be? How many dimes will be left over?

4. There are 20 Little League teams in the city. The League places 10 teams in a division. How many divisions will there be in the city? Write a number sentence for this story and all the number sentences in this fact family.

5. Write a story to show $45 \div 9$. Draw a picture to go with your story and write a number sentence. Write all the other number sentences that are in this fact family.

6. Show two ways you can have 25 cents if you have only dimes and nickels.

7. Show three ways you can have 40 cents if you have only dimes and nickels.

8. Chewy Candies come in packs of five. Irma has 3 packs, Michael has 5 packs, Romesh has 1 pack, and Jessie has no packs.

   A. How many candies does each student have? Write a number sentence for each student.

   B. How many candies do they have altogether?

9. Jacob has 60 cents and needs $1.00 for a show. How many dimes does he need to make $1.00?

10. A pack of Chewy Candies costs 15 cents. How many packs can you buy with $1.00? Explain your solution.

Multiplication Facts I Know

- Circle the facts you know well.
- Keep this table and use it to help you multiply.
- As you learn more facts, you may circle them too.

×	0	1	2	3	4	5	6	7	8	9	10
0	0	0	0	0	0	0	0	0	0	0	0
1	0	1	2	3	4	5	6	7	8	9	10
2	0	2	4	6	8	10	12	14	16	18	20
3	0	3	6	9	12	15	18	21	24	27	30
4	0	4	8	12	16	20	24	28	32	36	40
5	0	5	10	15	20	25	30	35	40	45	50
6	0	6	12	18	24	30	36	42	48	54	60
7	0	7	14	21	28	35	42	49	56	63	70
8	0	8	16	24	32	40	48	56	64	72	80
9	0	9	18	27	36	45	54	63	72	81	90
10	0	10	20	30	40	50	60	70	80	90	100

Daily Practice and Problems

Students may solve the items individually, in groups, or as a class. The items may also be assigned for homework.

Student Questions	Teacher Notes

3B Nickels

What is the value of:

1. 5 nickels?

2. 8 nickels?

3. 6 dimes?

4. 2 dimes and 6 nickels?

How many nickels in:

5. 15¢

6. 45¢

7. 20¢

8. 35¢

TIMS Task

1. 25¢   2. 40¢

3. 60¢   4. 50¢

5. 3   6. 9

7. 4   8. 7

3C Fact Families for × and ÷

Solve each pair of related facts. Then, name two other facts in the same fact family.

1. $5 \times 2 =$ $10 \div 2 =$

2. $5 \times 6 =$ $30 \div 6 =$

3. $5 \times 5 =$ $25 \div 5 =$

4. $10 \times 7 =$ $70 \div 7 =$

5. $10 \times 4 =$ $40 \div 10 =$

6. $10 \times 10 =$ $100 \div 10 =$

TIMS Bit

1. 10, 5, $2 \times 5 = 10$, $10 \div 5 = 2$

2. 30, 5, $6 \times 5 = 30$, $30 \div 5 = 6$

3. 25, 5, No other facts in this fact family; why?

4. 70, 10, $7 \times 10 = 70$, $70 \div 10 = 7$

5. 40, 4, $4 \times 10 = 40$, $40 \div 4 = 10$

6. 100, 10, No other facts in this fact family.

Student Questions	Teacher Notes

3E Time

1. Skip count by 5 minutes from 10:00 to 11:00.

2. Skip count by 10 minutes from 1:00 to 2:00.

3. How many minutes have gone by from 3:05 to 3:20?

4. How many minutes have gone by from 7:40 to 8:05?

3F Story Solving

A. Write a story to show 5×7. Draw a picture to go with your story. Write a number sentence on your picture.

B. Write a story and a number sentence to show $35 \div 7$.

C. What are the other two facts in this fact family?

Student Questions	Teacher Notes

3H Fingers and Toes

1. How many fingers are in the room right now? How many toes?

2. About how many fingers are in the school right now? About how many toes?

3. Explain how you solved Question 2.

4. There are 40 fingers around our table. How many hands are there? How many people?

TIMS Task

Answers will vary for Questions 1–3.

4. 8 hands
   4 people

3K Skip Counting

1. Start on 0 and skip count by 5s on the calculator for 15 seconds.

2. Start on 0 and skip count by 10s on the calculator for 15 seconds. How far did you get?

TIMS Bit

1–2. Students should work in pairs for this activity.
To skip count by fives on the calculator, students should press: 5 + 5 = = = = = , etc. Calculators with the constant feature will repeat the operation, in this case adding five, each time the equal sign is pressed. Could they count twice as far by 10s as by 5s?

3L Working with Fact Families for × and ÷

Solve the problems below and complete the number sentences for the related facts.

A. 5 × 10 = ___

___ ÷ 5 = ___

___ ÷ 10 = ___

___ × 5 = ___

B. 7 × 5 = ___

___ ÷ 7 = ___

___ ÷ 5 = ___

___ × 7 = ___

C. 3 × 10 = ___

___ ÷ 3 = ___

___ ÷ 10 = ___

___ × 10 = ___

D. 80 ÷ 8 = ___

___ × 8 = ___

80 ÷ ___ = ___

8 × ___ = ___

E. 20 ÷ 5 = ___

___ × 5 = ___

5 × ___ = ___

20 ÷ ___ = ___

F. 10 × 9 = ___

___ ÷ 9 = ___

___ ÷ ___ = 9

9 × ___ = ___

3M Quiz on 5s and 10s

A. 5 × 2 =   B. 3 × 10 =   C. 5 × 5 =

D. 8 × 10 =   E. 6 × 10 =   F. 5 × 3 =

G. 10 × 9 =   H. 7 × 5 =   I. 10 × 2 =

J. 10 × 7 =   K. 6 × 5 =   L. 5 × 10 =

M. 8 × 5 =   N. 9 × 5 =   O. 4 × 10 =

P. 4 × 5 =   Q. 10 × 10 =

TIMS Task

A. 5 × 10 = 50, 50 ÷ 5 = 10,
    50 ÷ 10 = 5, 10 × 5 = 50

B. 7 × 5 = 35, 35 ÷ 7 = 5,
    35 ÷ 5 = 7, 5 × 7 = 35

C. 3 × 10 = 30, 30 ÷ 3 = 10,
    30 ÷ 10 = 3, 3 × 10 = 30

D. 80 ÷ 8 = 10, 10 × 8 = 80,
    80 ÷ 10 = 8, 8 × 10 = 80

E. 20 ÷ 5 = 4, 4 × 5 = 20,
    5 × 4 = 20, 20 ÷ 4 = 5

F. 10 × 9 = 90, 90 ÷ 9 = 10,
    90 ÷ 10 = 9, 9 × 10 = 90

TIMS Bit

This quiz is on the first group of multiplication facts, the 5s and 10s. We recommend 2 minutes for this test. You might want to allow students to change pens after the time is up and complete the remaining problems in a different color.

After students take the test, have them update their *Multiplication Facts I Know* charts.

Unit 3: Home Practice

Part 1 *Triangle Flash Cards: 5s and 10s*

Study for the quiz on the multiplication facts for the fives and tens. Take home your *Triangle Flash Cards: 5s* and *10s* and your list of facts you need to study.

Here's how to use the flash cards. Ask a family member to choose one flash card at a time. He or she should cover the corner containing the highest number. This number will be the answer to a multiplication problem. Multiply the two uncovered numbers.

Study the math facts in small groups. Choose eight to ten facts to study each night. Your teacher will tell you when the quiz on the fives and tens will be.

Part 4 Fact Families

For each fact given, write the other three members of the same fact family.

A. $6 \times 5 = 30$

_____

_____

_____

B. $90 \div 10 = 9$

_____

_____

_____

C. $15 \div 5 = 3$

_____

_____

_____

D. $5 \times 9 = 45$

_____

_____

_____

E. $5 \times 10 = 50$

_____

_____

_____

Part 5 More Fact Families

Solve the problems below and complete the number sentences for the related facts.

A. $10 \times 10 =$ _____

_____ $\div 10 = 10$

B. $10 \div 5 =$ _____

_____ $\times 5 = 10$

$5 \times$ _____ $=$ _____

_____ $\div$ _____ $= 5$

C. _____ $\div 10 = 3$

_____ $\div 3 =$ _____

$3 \times$ _____ $=$ _____

_____ $\times 3 =$ _____

D. $6 \times$ _____ $= 30$

_____ $\times 6 =$ _____

$30 \div 6 =$ _____

$30 \div$ _____ $=$ _____

E. $7 \times 10 =$ _____

_____ $\times 7 =$ _____

_____ $\div 7 =$ _____

_____ $\div$ _____ $=$ _____

F. $1 \times 5 =$ _____

$5 \times$ _____ $=$ _____

$5 \div$ _____ $=$ _____

_____ $\div$ _____ $=$ _____

Facts Distribution
Multiplication and Division:
2s and 3s · Weeks 9-10

Math Facts Groups	Weeks	Daily Practice and Problems	Home Practice	Triangle Flash Cards	Facts Quizzes and Tests
Multiplication Review and Division Practice for the 2s and 3s	9–10	Unit 4: Items 4A–4C, 4E–4G, 4J–4M, 4R & 4S	Unit 4 Part 1	*Triangle Flash Cards: 2s* and *3s*	DPP Item 4S is a quiz on the 2s and 3s. The *Multiplication Facts I Know* chart is updated.

Students may solve the items individually, in groups, or as a class. The items may also be assigned for homework.

Student Questions	Teacher Notes

 Triangle Flash Cards: 2s and 3s

With a partner, use your *Triangle Flash Cards* to quiz each other on the multiplication facts involving twos and threes. One partner covers the shaded corner (containing the highest number). This number will be the answer to a multiplication fact called the product. The second person multiplies the two other numbers, one of which is circled and the other is in a square. These two are the factors.

Separate the used cards into three piles: those facts you know and can answer quickly, those that you can figure out with a strategy, and those that you need to learn. Practice the last two piles again and then make a list of the facts you need to practice at home for homework.

Circle the facts you know and can answer quickly on your *Multiplication Facts I Know* chart.

TIMS Bit

The *Triangle Flash Cards* follow the Home Practice for this unit in the *Discovery Assignment Book*. Part 1 of the Home Practice reminds students to bring home the list of the facts they need to practice for homework. The *Triangle Flash Cards* should also be sent home.

Have students circle the facts they know well on their *Multiplication Facts I Know* charts. Remind students that if they know a fact, they also know its turn-around fact. Since these charts can also be used as multiplication tables, students should have them available to use as needed.

Inform students when the quiz on the twos and threes will be given. This quiz appears in TIMS Bit S.

Pattern Triangle

Look at the triangle and answer the following questions.

1. Describe any patterns in the rows (across).

2. Do the diagonal columns show any patterns?

3. Complete the last row of the triangle.

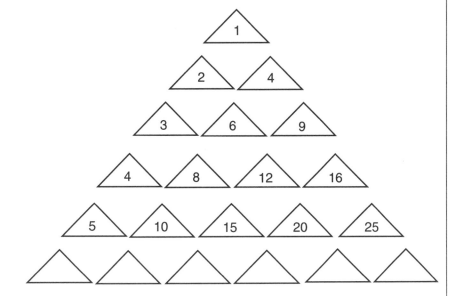

TIMS Task

1. Counting by 2s, 3s, 4s, then 5s; The third row has multiples of 3, etc.

2. First diagonal column moving down to the left is counting by ones, second column starts with 4 and counts on by twos, etc. The last or rightmost diagonal column moving down to the right is made up of square numbers. Students may see other patterns.

3. 6, 12, 18, 24, 30, 36

 Using Twos

Do these problems in your head. Write only the answers.

A. $2 \times 9 =$ B. $3 \times 200 =$

C. $2 \times 1000 =$ D. $8 \times 2 =$

E. $5 \times 20 =$ F. $20 \times 2 =$

G. $40 \times 2 =$ H. $6 \times 2 =$

I. $2 \times 7 =$ J. $0 \times 2 =$

TIMS Bit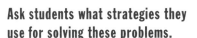

Ask students what strategies they use for solving these problems.

A. 18	B. 600
C. 2000	D. 16
E. 100	F. 40
G. 80	H. 12
I. 14	J. 0

4E Fact Families

Solve each pair of related facts. Then name two other facts in the same fact family.

1. $2 \times 6 =$ $12 \div 6 =$

2. $5 \times 3 =$ $3 \times 5 =$

3. $8 \times 2 =$ $16 \div 8 =$

4. $7 \times 3 =$ $3 \times 7 =$

5. $12 \div 4 =$ $4 \times 3 =$

4F Baseball Cards

Tim bought a notebook and a package of 65 plastic pages with pockets to hold his baseball cards. Each page had 3 rows of 3 pockets on the front side and another 3 rows of 3 pockets on the back side.

1. How many baseball cards did each page hold?

2. How many baseball cards could be held with all the pages?

TIMS Bit

1. 12, 2, $6 \times 2 = 12$, $12 \div 2 = 6$

2. 15, 15, $15 \div 5 = 3$, $15 \div 3 = 5$

3. 16, 2, $2 \times 8 = 16$, $16 \div 2 = 8$

4. 21, 21, $21 \div 3 = 7$, $21 \div 7 = 3$

5. 3, 12, $12 \div 3 = 4$, $3 \times 4 = 12$

TIMS Task

1. 18 cards

   $3 \times 3 = 9$ cards on the front side

   $3 \times 3 = 9$ cards on the back side

2. 1170 cards; Students will need calculators to solve this problem.

   18 cards $\times$ 65 pages = 1170 cards

4G Working with Fact Families for × and ÷

Solve the problems below and complete the number sentences for the related facts.

A. $2 \times 7 = $ _____

_____ $\div 2 = $ _____

_____ $\div 7 = $ _____

_____ $\times 2 = $ _____

B. $3 \times 9 = $ _____

_____ $\div 9 = $ _____

_____ $\div 3 = $ _____

_____ $\times 3 = $ _____

C. $3 \times 6 = $ _____

_____ $\div 3 = $ _____

_____ $\div 6 = $ _____

_____ $\times 3 = $ _____

D. $2 \times 4 = $ _____

_____ $\times 2 = $ _____

_____ $\div 4 = $ _____

_____ $\div 2 = $ _____

E. $2 \times 9 = $ _____

_____ $\div 9 = $ _____

$9 \times $ _____ $ = $ _____

_____ $\div 2 = $ _____

F. $8 \times 3 = $ _____

_____ $\div 8 = $ _____

_____ $\div 3 = $ _____

_____ $\times $ _____ $ = $ _____

G. $3 \times 10 = $ _____

_____ $\div 3 = $ _____

$10 \times $ _____ $ = $ _____

_____ $\div 10 = $ _____

H. $2 \times $ _____ $ = 20$

_____ $\div 2 = $ _____

$20 \div 10 = $ _____

$10 \times $ _____ $ = 20$

TIMS Bit

A. $2 \times 7 = 14, 14 \div 2 = 7,$
$14 \div 7 = 2, 7 \times 2 = 14$

B. $3 \times 9 = 27, 27 \div 9 = 3,$
$27 \div 3 = 9, 9 \times 3 = 27$

C. $3 \times 6 = 18, 18 \div 3 = 6,$
$18 \div 6 = 3, 6 \times 3 = 18$

D. $2 \times 4 = 8, 4 \times 2 = 8,$
$8 \div 4 = 2, 8 \div 2 = 4$

E. $2 \times 9 = 18, 18 \div 9 = 2,$
$9 \times 2 = 18, 18 \div 2 = 9$

F. $8 \times 3 = 24, 24 \div 8 = 3,$
$24 \div 3 = 8, 3 \times 8 = 24$

G. $3 \times 10 = 30, 30 \div 3 = 10,$
$10 \times 3 = 30, 30 \div 10 = 3$

H. $2 \times 10 = 20, 20 \div 2 = 10,$
$20 \div 10 = 2, 10 \times 2 = 20$

Student Questions	Teacher Notes

4J Going to the Movies

1. Roberto went to the movies on Saturday with his mother, father, and his 2 younger sisters. Tickets cost $6.00 for adults and $4.50 for children. How much did it cost the family to go to the movies?

2. Prices on Tuesdays are only $4.50 for adults and $3.00 for children. How much will Roberto's family save if they go to the movies on Tuesday instead of Saturday?

TIMS Task

1. One solution:
2 × $6.00 + 3 × $4.50 = $12.00 + $13.50 = $25.50

2. One way is to find the price on Tuesday and subtract:
2 × $4.50 + 3 × $3.00 = $9.00 + $9.00 = $18.00. They would have saved $25.50 − $18.00 = $7.50. Another way is to note that the prices for both adult and children's tickets are $1.50 less on Tuesday. Since they bought 5 tickets, they would have spent 5 × $1.50 = $7.50 less on Tuesday.

4K Multiples of a Number

1. Is 9 a multiple of 2? Why or why not?

2. Is 15 a multiple of 3? Why or why not?

3. Is 3 a factor of 18? Why or why not?

4. Is 2 a factor of 7? Why or why not?

5. Name three numbers greater than 21 that are multiples of 2.

6. Name three factors of 12.

TIMS Bit

1. No; Students may skip count: 2, 4, 6, 8, 10. Or, students may reason that a rectangle cannot be formed with 9 tiles using 2 tiles in each row. (Students build rectangles using square-inch tiles in Lesson 1.)

2. Yes; Students may skip count: 3, 6, 9, 12, 15. Students may say that 3 × 5 = 15. Others may say that a rectangle with 3 rows of 5 tiles can be formed. This rectangle would have 15 square-inch tiles.

3. Yes; 18 ÷ 3 = 6; 3 evenly divides 18; 6 is a whole number.

4. No; 7 ÷ 2 = 3.5; 3.5 is not a whole number.

5. Students may skip count until they reach beyond 21. Three possible answers are: 22, 24, 26.

6. Answers will vary. The factors of 12 are 1, 2, 3, 4, 6, 12.

Student Questions	Teacher Notes

 Tiling the Shower

Myrna Myrmidon and her Aunt Penny want to tile 3 walls of their shower. Each wall is 3 inches by 2 inches. How many square-inch tiles will they need in all? If the tiles come in packages of 10, how many packages should they buy?

TIMS Task

Students might think a shower 3 inches by 2 inches does not make sense. However, remind students that Myrna Myrmidon and Aunt Penny are two ants that live in Antopolis. They were introduced in Unit 2. Constructing runways for Antopolis Airport was the context for learning about area and perimeter.

Each of the three walls is 6 square inches.

Altogether, the three walls have a total area of 18 square inches.

They will need 2 boxes.

 Making Rectangles with Tiles

Make a table like the one below to show all the different rectangles that can be made with 54 tiles. You can use a calculator or multiplication facts to help you divide.

Number of Rows	Number in Each Row	Division Sentence
1	54	$54 \div 1 = 54$
2		$54 \div 2 =$

TIMS Bit

Possible rectangles are:

1×54, 2×27,

3×18, and 6×9

2	27	$54 \div 2 = 27$
3	18	$54 \div 3 = 18$
6	9	$54 \div 6 = 9$

Because of our agreement that we will consider rectangles to be the same if one can be turned to look just like the other, it is not necessary to list 9, 18, 27, and 54 rows of tiles. However, some students might prefer to make this complete list.

9	6	$54 \div 9 = 6$
18	3	$54 \div 18 = 3$
27	2	$54 \div 27 = 2$
54	1	$54 \div 54 = 1$

4R **What Numbers Are We?**

1. I am more than 50 and less than 60. Both my digits are the same. Who am I?

2. I am more than 2 × 45 and less than 2 × 50. If you skip count by 5s you will hit me. Who am I?

3. I am even. I am less than 3 × 6 but more than 3 × 5. Who am I?

4. Make up your own riddle. Write it down and trade with a friend. Can you solve your friend's riddle?

TIMS Task

1. 55

2. 95

3. 16

4. Answers will vary.

4S **Quiz on 2s and 3s**

A. 4 × 2 =	B. 3 × 2 =
C. 5 × 3 =	D. 2 × 10 =
E. 6 × 3 =	F. 2 × 5 =
G. 10 × 3 =	H. 7 × 2 =
I. 8 × 3 =	J. 3 × 3 =
K. 8 × 2 =	L. 2 × 2 =
M. 9 × 2 =	N. 6 × 2 =
O. 3 × 7 =	P. 4 × 3 =
Q. 3 × 9 =	R. 1 × 3 =

TIMS Bit

This quiz is on the second group of multiplication facts, the twos and threes. We recommend 2 minutes for this quiz. Allow students to change pens after the time is up and complete the remaining problems in a different color.

After students take the quiz, have them update their *Multiplication Facts I Know* charts.

Unit 4: Home Practice

Part 1 *Triangle Flash Cards: 2s and 3s*

Study for the quiz on the multiplication facts for the 2s and 3s. Take home your *Triangle Flash Cards: 2s* and *3s* and your list of facts you need to study.

Here's how to use the flash cards. Ask a family member to choose one flash card at a time. He or she should cover the corner containing the highest number. This number will be the answer to a multiplication fact. Multiply the two uncovered numbers.

Study the math facts in small groups. Choose eight to ten facts to study each night. Your teacher will tell you when the quiz on the 2s and 3s will be.

5 Facts Distribution
Multiplication and Division:
Square Numbers · Weeks 11-13

Math Facts Groups	Weeks	Daily Practice and Problems	Home Practice	Triangle Flash Cards	Facts Quizzes and Tests
Multiplication Review and Division Practice for the Square Numbers	11–13	Unit 5: Items 5A, 5B, 5G–5J, 5L, 5N, 5P, 5T & 5U	Unit 5 Part 1	*Triangle Flash Cards: Square Numbers*	DPP Item 5U is a quiz on the square numbers. The *Multiplication Facts I Know* chart is updated.

Weeks 11-13

Students may solve the items individually, in groups, or as a class. The items may also be assigned for homework.

Student Questions	Teacher Notes

 Triangle Flash Cards: Square Numbers

With a partner, use your *Triangle Flash Cards* to quiz each other on the multiplication facts for the square numbers. One partner covers the shaded corner containing the highest number. This number will be the answer to a multiplication fact called the product. The second person multiplies the other two numbers. These two are the factors.

Separate the used cards into three piles: those facts you know and can answer quickly, those that you can figure out with a strategy, and those that you need to learn. Practice the last two piles again and then make a list of the facts you need to practice at home for homework.

Circle the facts you know and can answer quickly on your *Multiplication Facts I Know* chart.

TIMS Bit

The *Triangle Flash Cards* follow the Home Practice for this unit in the *Discovery Assignment Book*. Part 1 of the Home Practice reminds students to bring the list of the facts they need to practice home for homework. The *Triangle Flash Cards* should also be sent home.

Have students circle the facts they know well on their *Multiplication Facts I Know* charts. Remind students that if they know a fact, they also know its turn-around fact. Since these charts can also be used as multiplication tables, students should have them available to use as needed.

Inform students when the quiz on the square numbers will be given. This quiz appears in TIMS Bit U.

5B Guess My Number

I am a multiple of 3.

2 is not one of my factors.

I am not a prime and I am not a square.

I am less than 20.

What number am I?

Explain your strategy.

TIMS Task

15

All multiples of 3: 3, 6, 9, 12, 15, 18, 21, 24, 27, 30, etc.

Eliminate factors of 2, leaving 3, 9, 15, 21, 27, etc.

Eliminate prime numbers and square numbers, leaving 15, 21, 27, etc.

Only one number above is less than 20: 15.

5G Using Exponents

A. $2^2 = ?$ B. $3^2 = ?$

C. $2^2 + 3^2 = ?$ D. $4^2 = ?$

E. $3^2 \times 5 = ?$ F. $2 \times 4^2 = ?$

TIMS Bit

Students should use exponents before they add or multiply. For example, $2^2 + 3^2 = 4 + 9 = 13$.

A. 4   B. 9

C. 13   D. 16

E. 45   F. 32

5H Number Puzzle

I am a square number less than 100.

I am a multiple of 2, but I am not a multiple of 8.

2 is not my only prime factor.

What number am I?

Explain your strategy.

TIMS Task

36

Square numbers less than 100: 1, 4, 9, 16, 25, 36, 49, 64, 81

Numbers from the list above that are multiples of 2, but not of 8: 4 and 36

The only prime factor of 4 is 2.

Prime factors of 36: 2 and 3, so the answer is 36.

Student Questions	Teacher Notes

5I Fact Families for the Square Numbers

The square numbers have only two facts in each fact family.

For example, the following two facts are in the same fact family.

$$2 \times 2 = 4 \quad \text{and} \quad 4 \div 2 = 2$$

Solve the fact given. Then, name the second fact that is in the same fact family.

1. $9 \times 9 =$ _____   2. $5 \times 5 =$ _____

3. $7 \times 7 =$ _____   4. $8 \times 8 =$ _____

5. $10 \times 10 =$ _____   6. $3 \times 3 =$ _____

7. $6 \times 6 =$ _____   8. $4 \times 4 =$ _____

9. $1 \times 1 =$ _____

TIMS Bit

1. $81; 81 \div 9 = 9$
2. $25; 25 \div 5 = 5$
3. $49; 49 \div 7 = 7$
4. $64; 64 \div 8 = 8$
5. $100; 100 \div 10 = 10$
6. $9; 9 \div 3 = 3$
7. $36; 36 \div 6 = 6$
8. $16; 16 \div 4 = 4$
9. $1; 1 \div 1 = 1$

5J Grocery Shopping

1. Paper towels cost 70¢ a roll. How much will 7 rolls cost?

2. Turkey sandwiches cost $2.50. How much will 3 sandwiches cost?

3. Frozen yogurt cups cost 59¢ apiece. About how much will 6 cups cost?

4. A juice pack has 3 juice boxes. A juice pack costs $0.90. How much is each juice box worth?

TIMS Task

1. $4.90
2. $7.50
3. About $3.60
4. $0.30

Student Questions	Teacher Notes

5L Area and Perimeter

1. Imagine a rectangle with 7 rows of square-inch tiles. Each row has 7 tiles in it.

   A. What is the area of this rectangle?

   B. What is the perimeter? Make a sketch of this rectangle.

2. Imagine a square with perimeter of 32 inches. What is the area of this square? Make a sketch of this square.

TIMS Task

1. A. 49 square inches

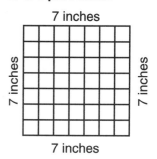

B. 28 inches

2. 64 square inches

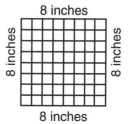

5N Square Numbers

Find a number for *n* that makes each sentence true.

1. $n \times n = 81$ $n = $ _____

2. $n \times n = 36$ $n = $ _____

3. $n \times n = 49$ $n = $ _____

4. $n \times n = 25$ $n = $ _____

5. $n \times n = 9$ $n = $ _____

6. $n \times n = 64$ $n = $ _____

7. $n \times n = 16$ $n = $ _____

8. $n \times n = 1$ $n = $ _____

9. $n \times n = 4$ $n = $ _____

TIMS Task

Explain to students that in each sentence both *n*s have to have the same value.

1. $n = 9$

2. $n = 6$

3. $n = 7$

4. $n = 5$

5. $n = 3$

6. $n = 8$

7. $n = 4$

8. $n = 1$

9. $n = 2$

5P Another Number Puzzle

I am a number between 6 and 150.

I am one more than a square number.

The sum of my digits is a multiple of 5.

I am prime.

What number am I?

Explain your strategy.

TIMS Challenge N

37

Square numbers between 6–150: 9, 16, 25, 36, 49, 64, 81, 100, 121, 144

Numbers one larger than the squares above (between 6 and 150): 10, 17, 26, 37, 50, 65, 82, 101, 122, 145

Numbers from the list above whose digits sum to a multiple of five:

37 (3 + 7 = 10),

50 (5 + 0 = 5),

82, 122, 145

Of these numbers, only 37 is a prime number. The others are divisible by 2 or 5.

5T Missing Factors

m and n stand for missing numbers. Find the missing numbers in each of the following.

1. $2 \times m = 4$

2. $m \times 8 = 24$

3. $6 \times m = 36$

4. $10 \times m = 100$

5. $64 \div m = 8$

6. $81 \div 9 = m$

7. $4 \times n = 16$

8. $m \times n = 11$

9. $m^2 = 25$

TIMS Task N

1. 2   2. 3

3. 6   4. 10

5. 8   6. 9

7. 4   8. 1, 11

9. 5

5U Quiz on the Square Numbers

A. $4 \times 4 =$ B. $7 \times 7 =$

C. $2 \times 2 =$ D. $10 \times 10 =$

E. $3 \times 3 =$ F. $5 \times 5 =$

G. $6 \times 6 =$ H. $8 \times 8 =$

I. $9 \times 9 =$ J. $1 \times 1 =$

TIMS Bit

This quiz is on the third group of multiplication facts, the square numbers. We recommend 1 minute for this test. Allow students to change pens after the time is up and complete the remaining problems in a different color.

After students take the test, have them update their *Multiplication Facts I Know* charts.

Unit 5: Home Practice

Part 1 *Triangle Flash Cards: Square Numbers*

Study for the quiz on the multiplication facts for the square numbers.
Take home your *Triangle Flash Cards: Square Numbers* and your list of
facts you need to study.

Here's how to use the flash cards. Ask a family member to choose one flash
card at a time. Your helper should cover the corner containing the highest number.
This number will be the answer to a multiplication fact. Multiply the two uncovered
numbers.

Your teacher will tell you when the quiz on the square numbers will be.

5

Facts Distribution
Multiplication and Division:
9s · Weeks 14-15

Math Facts Groups	Weeks	Daily Practice and Problems	Home Practice	Triangle Flash Cards	Facts Quizzes and Tests
Multiplication Review and Division Practice for the 9s	14–15	Unit 6: Items 6A, 6C, 6G, 6H, 6J–6M & 6O	Unit 6 Parts 1 & 2	*Triangle Flash Cards: 9s*	DPP Item 6O is a quiz on the 9s. The *Multiplication Facts I Know* chart is updated.

Students may solve the items individually, in groups, or as a class. The items may also be assigned for homework.

Student Questions	Teacher Notes

 Triangle Flash Cards: 9s

With a partner, use your *Triangle Flash Cards* to quiz each other on the multiplication facts for the nines. One partner covers the shaded corner containing the highest number. This number will be the answer to a multiplication fact, called the product. The second person multiplies the other two numbers, one of which is in a circle and the other is in a square. These two are the factors.

Separate the used cards into three piles: those facts you know and can answer quickly, those that you can figure out with a strategy, and those that you need to learn. Practice the last two piles again and then make a list of the facts you need to practice at home for homework.

Circle the facts you know quickly on your *Multiplication Facts I Know* chart.

TIMS Bit

The *Triangle Flash Cards* follow the Home Practice in the *Discovery Assignment Book.* Part 1 of the Home Practice reminds students to bring home the list of the facts they need to practice for homework. The *Triangle Flash Cards* should also be sent home.

Have students circle the facts they know well on their *Multiplication Facts I Know* charts. Remind students that if they know a fact, they also know its turn-around fact. Since these charts can also be used as multiplication tables, students should have them available to use as needed.

Inform students when the quiz on the 9s will be given. This quiz appears in TIMS Bit O.

6C Patterns

Complete:

1 × 9 =

2 × 9 =

3 × 9 =

4 × 9 =

5 × 9 =

6 × 9 =

7 × 9 =

8 × 9 =

9 × 9 =

10 × 9 =

What patterns do you see?

TIMS Bit

Observing patterns helps students remember the facts for the nines. Patterns include:

1. When products are listed in a column, the digits in the tens' place count up by ones (0, 1, 2, 3, . . .) and the digits in the ones' place count down by ones (9, 8, 7, . . .).

2. The sum of the digits in each product is nine. For example, 36 is the product of 4 × 9. The sum of 3 and 6 is nine. This provides a strategy for checking multiplication by nine: Does 9 × 6 = 54 or 56? It must be 54 since 5 + 4 = 9, but 5 + 6 is not 9.

3. The nines can be easily derived from the tens. For example, 10 × 4 is 40. So, 9 × 4 is 4 less: 40 − 4 = 36.

6G Nines Are Fine

Do these problems in your head. Write only the answers. Write a division number sentence in the same fact family for each one.

A. $9 \times 5 =$

B. $9 \times 7 =$

C. $8 \times 9 =$

D. $9 \times 2 =$

E. $6 \times 9 =$

F. $9 \times 4 =$

G. $10 \times 9 =$

H. $9 \times 9 =$

I. $9 \times 3 =$

J. $1 \times 9 =$

TIMS Bit

Ask students what strategies they use to solve these problems. One possible strategy for finding nine times a number is to multiply the number by ten, then subtract the number from the total. (Example: $9 \times 6 = 10 \times 6 - 6$.) See Bit C for more strategies.

A. 45	B. 63
C. 72	D. 18
E. 54	F. 36
G. 90	H. 81
I. 27	J. 9

Answers will vary for the division sentences.

6H Calculator Counting

1. Use a calculator to count by 3s to 100. Work with a partner. One partner will count, saying the numbers quietly. The other partner will time how long the counting takes. Take turns. How long did it take? Can you land on 100?

2. Use the data from Question 1 to predict how long it would take to count by 9s to 100. Then, use a calculator to count by 9s to 100. How long did it take? Can you land on 100?

TIMS Task

Students may work in groups of two for this activity. To skip count by 3s on a calculator with a constant function, students press:

Did students count three times as fast by 9s as by 3s? Since 100 is not a multiple of 3 or 9, you cannot land on 100 when skip counting by 3 or 9.

Mr. and Mrs. Head

Mr. Head says that 9 × 5 = 46, and Mrs. Head cannot convince him he's wrong. Write a letter to Mr. Head explaining what 9 × 5 equals and why. You may use drawings in your letter.

TIMS Task

Possible solutions include skip counting, drawing pictures of 9 groups of 5 things, drawing a 9 × 5 array, and reasoning that since 10 × 5 is 50 and 9 × 5 is 5 less, 9 × 5 must be 45. Or, since the sum of the digits of 46 is not 9 (4 + 6 ≠ 9), then 9 × 5 cannot equal 46. Also, all multiples of 5 end in 5 or 0; thus 46 is not a possible product.

6K **Fact Families for × and ÷**

Complete the number sentences for the related facts.

A. $3 \times 9 =$ ____

    ____ $\div 3 =$ ____

    ____ $\div 9 =$ ____

    ____ $\times 3 =$ ____

B. $9 \times 7 =$ ____

    ____ $\div 7 =$ ____

    ____ $\div 9 =$ ____

    $7 \times$ ____ $=$ ____

C. $9 \times 9 =$ ____

    ____ $\div 9 =$ ____

D. $54 \div 9 =$ ____

    $9 \times$ ____ $= 54$

    $54 \div$ ____ $= 9$

    ____ $\times 9 =$ ____

E. $9 \times 4 =$ ____

    ____ $\div 9 = 4$

    ____ $\div 4 =$ ____

    ____ $\times 9 =$ ____

A. 27; 27 ÷ 3 = 9;
   27 ÷ 9 = 3;
   9 × 3 = 27

B. 63; 63 ÷ 7 = 9;
   63 ÷ 9 = 7;
   7 × 9 = 63

C. 81; 81 ÷ 9 = 9

D. 6; 9 × 6 = 54;
   54 ÷ 6 = 9;
   6 × 9 = 54

E. 36; 36 ÷ 9 = 4;
   36 ÷ 4 = 9;
   4 × 9 = 36

6L Who Am I?

1. I am a square number greater than 9. One of my two digits is 5 more than the other. Who am I?

2. I am a square number less than 100. One of my digits is 8 less than twice the other. Who am I?

3. Make up your own square number riddle and try it on a partner.

TIMS Challenge

Answers will vary.

1. 16 or 49

2. 25 or 64

3. Answers will vary. Have some students present their riddles to the whole class.

6M More Fine Nines

Do these problems in your head. Write the answers and then write the other number sentences in the same fact family.

A. $9 \times 3 =$

B. $9 \times 2 =$

C. $63 \div 9 =$

D. $8 \times 9 =$

E. $81 \div 9 =$

F. $9 \times 4 =$

G. $10 \times 9 =$

H. $54 \div 9 =$

I. $5 \times 9 =$

TIMS Bit

Ask students what strategies they use to solve these problems.

A. 27; $3 \times 9 = 27$; $27 \div 9 = 3$; $27 \div 3 = 9$

B. 18; $2 \times 9 = 18$; $18 \div 9 = 2$; $18 \div 2 = 9$

C. 7; $63 \div 7 = 9$; $7 \times 9 = 63$; $9 \times 7 = 63$

D. 72; $9 \times 8 = 72$; $72 \div 9 = 8$; $72 \div 8 = 9$

E. 9; $9 \times 9 = 81$

F. 36; $4 \times 9 = 36$; $36 \div 4 = 9$; $36 \div 9 = 4$

G. 90; $9 \times 10 = 90$; $90 \div 9 = 10$; $90 \div 10 = 9$

H. 6; $54 \div 6 = 9$; $6 \times 9 = 54$; $9 \times 6 = 54$

I. 45; $9 \times 5 = 45$; $45 \div 9 = 5$; $45 \div 5 = 9$

60 Multiplication Quiz: 9s

A. $3 \times 9 =$ B. $9 \times 7 =$

C. $10 \times 9 =$ D. $2 \times 9 =$

E. $5 \times 9 =$ F. $9 \times 8 =$

G. $6 \times 9 =$ H. $4 \times 9 =$

I. $9 \times 9 =$ J. $9 \times 1 =$

TIMS Bit

This quiz is on the fourth group of multiplication facts, the nines. We recommend 2 minutes for this quiz. Allow students to change pens after the time is up and complete the remaining problems in a different color.

After students take the test, have them update their *Multiplication Facts I Know* charts.

Unit 6: Home Practice

Part 1 *Triangle Flash Cards: 9s*

Study for the quiz on the multiplication facts for the nines. Take home your *Triangle Flash Cards: 9s* and your list of facts you need to study.

Here's how to use the flash cards. Ask a family member to choose one flash card at a time. He or she should cover the corner containing the highest number. This number will be the answer to a multiplication fact. Multiply the two uncovered numbers.

Your teacher will tell you when the quiz on the 9s will be.

Part 2 **Mixed-Up Multiplication Tables**

1. Complete the table. Then, describe any patterns you see.

×	2	3	5	9	10
4					
6		18			
7					
8					

2. *n* stands for a missing number. Find the missing number in each number sentence.

   A. $n \times 7 = 14$ **B.** $3 \times n = 24$ **C.** $n \times 4 = 16$ **D.** $n \times 8 = 80$

   E. $9 \times n = 63$ **F.** $n \times 8 = 64$ **G.** $4 \times n = 36$ **H.** $n \times 5 = 30$

Facts Distribution
Multiplication and Division:
The Last Six Facts · Weeks 16-18

Math Facts Groups	Weeks	Daily Practice and Problems	Home Practice	Triangle Flash Cards	Facts Quizzes and Tests
Multiplication Review and Division Practice for The Last Six Facts	16–18	Unit 7: Items 7A, 7B, 7E–7H, 7J, 7M–7O, 7Y & 7AA	Unit 7 Parts 1 & 5	*Triangle Flash Cards: The Last Six Facts*	DPP Item 7AA is a quiz on The Last Six Facts. *The Multiplication Facts I Know* chart is updated.

Daily Practice and Problems

Students may solve the items individually, in groups, or as a class. The items may also be assigned for homework.

Student Questions	Teacher Notes

7A *Triangle Flash Cards: Last Six Facts*

With a partner, use your *Triangle Flash Cards* to quiz each other on the multiplication facts for the last six facts. One partner covers the shaded corner containing the highest number. The second person multiplies the two uncovered numbers. These two are the factors.

Separate the used cards into three piles: those facts you know and can answer quickly, those that you can figure out with a strategy, and those that you need to learn. Practice the last two piles again and then make a list of the facts you need to practice at home for homework.

Circle the facts you know quickly on your *Multiplication Facts I Know* chart.

TIMS Bit

The *Triangle Flash Cards* follow the Home Practice for this unit in the *Discovery Assignment Book*. Part 1 of the Home Practice reminds students to bring home the list of facts they need to practice for homework. The *Triangle Flash Cards* should also be sent home.

Have students record the facts they know well on their *Multiplication Facts I Know* charts. Students should circle the facts they know and can answer quickly. Since these charts can also be used as multiplication tables, students should have them available to use as needed.

Inform students when the quiz on the last six facts will be given. This quiz appears in TIMS Bit AA.

Fact Families for × and ÷

Complete the number sentences for the related facts.

A. $4 \times 7 =$ ___

    ___ $\div 4 =$ ___

    ___ $\div 7 =$ ___

    ___ $\times 4 =$ ___

B. $8 \times 6 =$ ___

    ___ $\div 8 =$ ___

    ___ $\div 6 =$ ___

    $6 \times$ ___ $=$ ___

C. $6 \times 7 =$ ___

    ___ $\div 6 =$ ___

    ___ $\div 7 =$ ___

    ___ $\times 6 =$ ___

D. $24 \div 6 =$ ___

    ___ $\times 6 =$ ___

    $24 \div$ ___ $=$ ___

    ___ $\times 4 =$ ___

E. $8 \times 7 =$ ___

    ___ $\div 8 =$ ___

    ___ $\div 7 =$ ___

    ___ $\times 8 =$ ___

F. $32 \div 8 =$ ___

    $4 \times$ ___ $=$ ___

    ___ $\div 4 =$ ___

    ___ $\times 4 =$ ___

TIMS Task

A. 28; $28 \div 4 = 7$
      $28 \div 7 = 4$
      $7 \times 4 = 28$

B. 48; $48 \div 8 = 6$
      $48 \div 6 = 8$
      $6 \times 8 = 48$

C. 42; $42 \div 6 = 7$
      $42 \div 7 = 6$
      $7 \times 6 = 42$

D. 4; $4 \times 6 = 24$
      $24 \div 4 = 6$
      $6 \times 4 = 24$

E. 56; $56 \div 8 = 7$
      $56 \div 7 = 8$
      $7 \times 8 = 56$

F. 4; $4 \times 8 = 32$
      $32 \div 4 = 8$
      $8 \times 4 = 32$

7E **Doubles**

1. A. $2 \times 6 =$

    B. $12 + 12 =$

    C. $4 \times 6 =$

2. A. $2 \times 7 =$

    B. $14 + 14 =$

    C. $4 \times 7 =$

3. A. $2 \times 8 =$

    B. $16 + 16 =$

    C. $4 \times 8 =$

What patterns do you see? Describe a strategy for multiplying a number by 4.

TIMS Bit

1. A. 12

    B. 24

    C. 24

2. A. 14

    B. 28

    C. 28

3. A. 16

    B. 32

    C. 32

One strategy for multiplying a number by 4 is to multiply first by 2. Then, double the answer. These problems are designed to help students see this pattern. Ask students if they have other patterns for finding the answers to these fact problems.

7F Break Apart Sevens

One way to solve 8 × 7 is to break the 7 into 5 + 2.

$8 \times 5 = 40$ $8 \times 2 = 16$

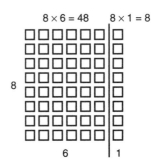

8

5 | 2

$8 \times 7 = 40 + 16 = 56$

$8 \times 5 = 40$ and $8 \times 2 = 16$,
so $8 \times 7 = 40 + 16 = 56$

1. Draw a picture for 8 × 7 that uses 7 broken into 4 + 3. Write a number sentence that goes with your picture.

2. Find another way to break up 7. Draw a picture. Write a number sentence for this picture.

3. Write the four number sentences in the fact family for 8 × 7.

TIMS Task

1. $8 \times 4 = 32$ $8 \times 3 = 24$

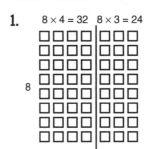

8

4 | 3

$8 \times 7 = 32 + 24 = 56$

2. Another way to break up 7 is to use 6 + 1.

$8 \times 6 = 48$ $8 \times 1 = 8$

8

6 | 1

$8 \times 7 = 48 + 8 = 56$

3. $8 \times 7 = 56$
   $7 \times 8 = 56$
   $56 \div 8 = 7$
   $56 \div 7 = 8$

7G Order of Operations

TIMS Bit

Remember the order of operations as you do the following problems. Do these problems mentally or with pencil and paper, not calculators.

A. 15 + 5 = 20

B. 6 + 5 = 11

C. 9 + 48 = 57

D. 3 + 42 = 45

E. 32 + 2 = 34

F. 10 − 9 = 1

A. $3 \times 5 + 5 =$ B. $6 + 20 \div 4 =$

C. $9 + 8 \times 6 =$ D. $6 \div 2 + 7 \times 6 =$

E. $4 \times 8 + 1 \times 2 =$

F. $10 - 3 \times 3 =$

7H *Operation Target:* 1, 3, 6, 9

TIMS Challenge

Play *Operation Target.*

- Use the four digits 1, 3, 6, 9, and the four operations (+, −, ×, ÷) to make as many numbers as you can.

- In each number sentence, you must use each of the four digits exactly once.

- Use any operation more than once or not at all.

- You can make 2-digit numbers by putting two digits together.

- No fractions or decimals are allowed.

For example: $1 + 63 \div 9 = 8$

1. What is the largest number you can make?

2. What is the smallest number you can make?

3. Make the numbers 1 to 10.

1. $91 \times 63 = 5733$

2. $9 \times 1 - 6 - 3 = 0$

3. Answers will vary.
   $1 = 9 - 6 - 3 + 1$
   $2 = 6 \times 3 \div 9 \times 1$
   $3 = 6 \times 3 \div 9 + 1$
   $4 = 36 \div 9 \times 1$
   $5 = 36 \div 9 + 1$
   $6 = 9 - 6 \div 3 - 1$
   $7 = 9 - 6 \div 3 \times 1$
   $8 = 9 - 6 \div 3 + 1$
   $9 = 9 \div 3 \div 1 + 6$
   $10 = 6 \times 3 - 9 + 1$

7J **Story Solving**

Write a story for 6×8. Draw a picture for your story and label it with a number sentence.

 TIMS Task

Students' stories will vary.

7M **More Doubles**

1. A. $3 \times 7 =$

   B. $21 + 21 =$

   C. $6 \times 7 =$

2. A. $3 \times 8 =$

   B. $24 + 24 =$

   C. $6 \times 8 =$

3. A. $3 \times 4 =$

   B. $12 + 12 =$

   C. $6 \times 4 =$

What patterns do you see? Describe a strategy for multiplying a number by 6.

 TIMS Bit

1. A. 21
   B. 42
   C. 42
2. A. 24
   B. 48
   C. 48
3. A. 12
   B. 24
   C. 24

One strategy for multiplying a number by 6 is to multiply first by 3. Then, double the answer. These problems are designed to help students see this pattern. Ask students if they have other patterns for finding the answers to these fact problems.

7N Break Apart Eights

One way to solve 6 × 8 is to break the 8 into 5 + 3.

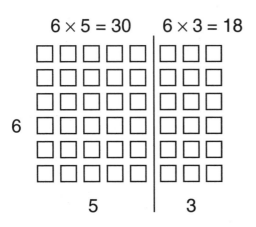

6 × 5 = 30   6 × 3 = 18

6

5   3

6 × 8 = 30 + 18 = 48

6 × 5 = 30 and 6 × 3 = 18, so
6 × 8 = 30 + 18 = 48

1. Draw a picture for 6 × 8 that uses 8 broken into 7 + 1.

2. Find another way to break up 8. Draw a picture. Write a number sentence for this picture.

3. Write the four number sentences in the fact family for 6 × 8.

TIMS Task

1.

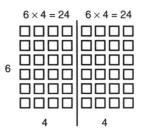

6 × 7 = 42   6 × 1 = 6

6

7   1

6 × 8 = 42 + 6 = 48

2. Another way to break up 8 is to use 4 + 4.

6 × 4 = 24   6 × 4 = 24

6

4   4

6 × 8 = 24 + 24 = 48

3. 6 × 8 = 48
   8 × 6 = 48
   48 ÷ 6 = 8
   48 ÷ 8 = 6

1O Multiplying by 10

Do these problems in your head.

A. 7 × 80 =

B. 6 × 400 =

C. 8000 × 6 =

D. 700 × 4 =

E. n × 60 = 420

F. 800 × n = 3200

G. 10 × 700 =

H. 0 × 600 =

TIMS Bit

In Lesson 4, students discuss patterns in multiplying numbers by multiples of 10.

A. 560   B. 2400

C. 48,000   D. 2800

E. 7   F. 4

G. 7000   H. 0

Student Questions	Teacher Notes

7Y Multiplying by Multiples of 10

A. $600 \times 4 =$ B. $8000 \times 7 =$

C. $4 \times 70 =$ D. $800 \times 6 =$

E. $8 \times 4000 =$ F. $600 \times 7 =$

TIMS Bit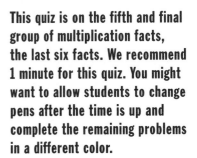

A. 2400   B. 56,000

C. 280   D. 4800

E. 32,000   F. 4200

7AA Multiplication Quiz: Last Six Facts

A. $8 \times 6 =$

B. $6 \times 4 =$

C. $4 \times 7 =$

D. $7 \times 8 =$

E. $6 \times 7 =$

F. $8 \times 4 =$

TIMS Bit

This quiz is on the fifth and final group of multiplication facts, the last six facts. We recommend 1 minute for this quiz. You might want to allow students to change pens after the time is up and complete the remaining problems in a different color.

After students take the test, have them update their *Multiplication Facts I Know* charts.

Unit 7: Home Practice

Part 1 *Triangle Flash Cards: Last Six Facts*

Study for the quiz on the multiplication facts for the last six facts. Take home your *Triangle Flash Cards: Last Six Facts* and your list of facts you need to study.

Here's how to use the flash cards. Ask a family member to choose one flash card at a time. Your partner should cover the corner containing the highest number. This number will be the answer to a multiplication fact. Multiply the two uncovered numbers.

Your teacher will tell you when the quiz on the last six facts will be.

Part 5 Multiplying by 10

1. Solve the following problems.

A. $6 \times 70 =$ _____   **B.** $8 \times 400 =$ _____

C. $800 \times 6 =$ _____   **D.** $7000 \times 4 =$ _____

E. $800 \times 8 =$ _____   **F.** $60 \times 4 =$ _____

2. Find what *n* must be to make each number sentence true.

A. $60 \times n = 360$ **B.** $n \times 5 = 350$ **C.** $n \times 900 = 5400$

Facts Distribution
Multiplication and Division:
Review All Fact Groups · Weeks 19-20

Math Facts Groups	Weeks	Daily Practice and Problems	Home Practice	Triangle Flash Cards	Facts Quizzes and Tests
Multiplication Assessment and Division Practice for All Fact Groups	19–20	Unit 8: Items 8A, 8E–8G, 8I, 8M, 8S, 8U & 8V The lesson *Facts I Know: Multiplication and Division Facts* (Unit 8 Lesson 8) begins the review and assessment of the division facts.	Unit 8 Part 1	*Triangle Flash Cards: 5s, 10s, 2s, 3s, Square Numbers, 9s,* and *The Last Six Facts*	DPP Item 8U is an inventory test on all five groups of multiplication facts. The *Multiplication Facts I Know* chart is updated.

Students may solve the items individually, in groups, or as a class. The items may also be assigned for homework.

Student Questions	Teacher Notes

8A Mixed-Up Multiplication Table

Complete the table. Look for patterns.

×	2	4	6	8	10
3					
5		20			
7					
9					

TIMS Bit   N $\frac{5}{\times 7}$

An inventory test on all of the multiplication facts is given in Bit U in Lesson 8. Tell students when the test will be administered. Part 1 of the Home Practice reminds students to take home their *Triangle Flash Cards* so they can study for the test. Alternatively, students may use the two copies of the *Triangle Flash Cards Master* that follow the Home Practice to make cards for those facts that have not yet been circled on their *Multiplication Facts I Know* charts. Encourage students to study the facts in small groups (8–10 facts at one time) and to focus especially on those facts they do not know or cannot answer quickly.

×	2	4	6	8	10
3	6	12	18	24	30
5	10	20	30	40	50
7	14	28	42	56	70
9	18	36	54	72	90

8E Fact Practice

Find the number for *n* that will make each number sentence true. Then write the other number sentences in that fact family.

A. $n \times 7 = 35$ B. $12 \div n = 2$

C. $12 \div n = 4$ D. $8 \times n = 32$

E. $9 \times n = 63$ F. $36 \div n = 6$

G. $40 \div n = 5$ H. $7 \times n = 49$

I. $30 \div n = 6$ J. $n \times 8 = 48$

TIMS Bit

A. $n = 5$
  $7 \times 5 = 35$
  $35 \div 7 = 5$
  $35 \div 5 = 7$

B. $n = 6$
  $12 \div 2 = 6$
  $2 \times 6 = 12$
  $6 \times 2 = 12$

C. $n = 3$
  $12 \div 4 = 3$
  $4 \times 3 = 12$
  $3 \times 4 = 12$

D. $n = 4$
  $4 \times 8 = 32$
  $32 \div 8 = 4$
  $32 \div 4 = 8$

E. $n = 7$
  $7 \times 9 = 63$
  $63 \div 7 = 9$
  $63 \div 9 = 7$

F. $n = 6$
  $6 \times 6 = 36$

G. $n = 8$
  $40 \div 5 = 8$
  $8 \times 5 = 40$
  $5 \times 8 = 40$

H. $n = 7$
  $49 \div 7 = 7$

I. $n = 5$
  $30 \div 6 = 5$
  $6 \times 5 = 30$
  $5 \times 6 = 30$

J. $n = 6$
  $8 \times 6 = 48$
  $48 \div 6 = 8$
  $48 \div 8 = 6$

8F Order of Operations

Irma and Jacob are playing *Operation Target.*

1. They recorded these number sentences using 4, 5, 6, and 8. Find the numbers they made.

    A. $4 + 6 + 5 \times 8 =$

    B. $6 \times 8 + 4 \times 5 =$

    C. $6 - 8 \div 4 + 5 =$

    D. $5 + 48 \div 6 =$

2. What is the largest whole number you can make with 4, 5, 6, 8 and one or more of the four operations $(+, -, \times, \div)$?

3. What is the smallest whole number you can make?

TIMS Task

Students were introduced to the game *Operation Target* in Unit 7 Lesson 1. Students may refer back to their *Student Guide* pages. In Lesson 2 of this unit, students played a new version of the game.

1. A. 50

    B. 68

    C. 9

    D. 13

2. $84 \times 65 = 5460$

3. $1; 8 + 4 - 5 - 6$

8G Counting Backwards

1. Use your calculator to subtract 4 over and over again from 36.

    Will zero ever be in the display? Why or why not? Try it.

2. Subtract 5 over and over again from 36.

    Will zero ever be in the display? Why or why not? Try it.

3. Subtract 9 over and over again from 36.

    Will zero ever be in the display? Why or why not? Try it.

TIMS Bit

Pressing $36 - 4 = = =$ on a calculator with a constant feature will cause the calculator to repeatedly subtract four.

1. Yes, because $36 \div 4 = 9$. Repeated subtraction is like division. Since the quotient of 36 and 4 is a whole number, 36 is divisible by 4 or 4 is a factor of 36.

2. No, because 36 is not divisible by 5.

3. Yes, because $36 \div 9 = 4$.

8I Estimation

1. Find the following products in your head.

   A. 90 × 40   B. 6000 × 90

   C. 50 × 400   D. 10 × 300

2. Use convenient numbers to estimate the products.

   A. 41 × 70   B. 79 × 82

   C. 2 × 797   D. 81 × 98

1. A. 3600
   B. 540,000
   C. 20,000
   D. 3000

2. A. Answers will vary.
      40 × 70 = 2800
   B. Answers will vary.
      80 × 80 = 6400
   C. Answers will vary.
      2 × 800 = 1600
   D. Answers will vary.
      80 × 100 = 8000

8M Facts Practice

TIMS Bit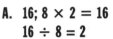

Solve the given fact. Then, name the other related fact or facts in the same fact family.

A. 2 × 8 = _____   B. 64 ÷ 8 = _____

C. 24 ÷ 6 = _____   D. 5 × 9 = _____

E. 4 × 4 = _____   F. 63 ÷ 9 = _____

G. 7 × 3 = _____   H. 27 ÷ 3 = _____

A. 16; 8 × 2 = 16
   16 ÷ 8 = 2
   16 ÷ 2 = 8

B. 8; 8 × 8 = 64

C. 4; 24 ÷ 4 = 6
   4 × 6 = 24
   6 × 4 = 24

D. 45; 9 × 5 = 45
   45 ÷ 5 = 9
   45 ÷ 9 = 5

E. 16; 16 ÷ 4 = 4

F. 7; 63 ÷ 7 = 9
   9 × 7 = 63
   7 × 9 = 63

G. 21; 3 × 7 = 21
   21 ÷ 3 = 7
   21 ÷ 7 = 3

H. 9; 27 ÷ 9 = 3
   3 × 9 = 27
   9 × 3 = 27

8§ Multiplication Facts

Emma has baked a cake. Here is a square to represent Emma's cake.

A. Show all the ways she can cut the cake if she wants to make 24 equal pieces. Write multiplication number sentences to describe each way.

B. Show all the ways she can cut the cake if she wants to make 30 equal pieces. Write multiplication number sentences to describe each way.

TIMS Bit

For each question discuss which ways of cutting the cake would be best and why. Have students demonstrate on the overhead projector or on the blackboard the various ways the cake can be cut. Have them use their drawings to justify their choices for the best way of cutting the cake. Note that turn-around facts will result in the same pieces.

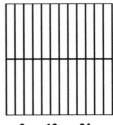

$2 \times 12 = 24$

A. $1 \times 24 = 24$, $2 \times 12 = 24$, $3 \times 8 = 24$, $4 \times 6 = 24$

B. $1 \times 30 = 30$, $2 \times 15 = 30$, $3 \times 10 = 30$, $5 \times 6 = 30$

8U Multiplication Facts Inventory Test

Students take the *Multiplication Facts Inventory Test.* It contains the multiplication facts from all five groups: 5s and 10s, 2s and 3s, square numbers, 9s, and the last six facts.

We recommend allowing four minutes for this test. Students should have two pens or pencils of different colors ready. During the first four minutes of the test, students write their answers using one color pen or pencil. Encourage students to answer first all the facts they know well and can answer quickly. Then, they should go back and use strategies to solve the rest. After you tell students that four minutes have passed, give them more time to complete the remaining items with the other color pen or pencil.

Students update their *Multiplication Facts I Know* charts using the results of the test.

TIMS Bit

The test can be found on the following page. It includes all the basic multiplication facts. Using their results of the test, students circle the facts they know and can answer quickly on their *Multiplication Facts I Know* charts. Then, students discuss strategies for figuring out or remembering any remaining facts that they do not know well. They can record these strategies in their journals.

A second inventory test will be given in Unit 16 for the division facts.

Name _____   Date _____

Multiplication Facts
Inventory Test

You will need two pens or pencils of different colors. Use the first color when you begin the test. When your teacher tells you to switch pens, finish the test using the second color.

9 $\times 2$	7 $\times 8$	10 $\times 4$	5 $\times 2$	8 $\times 4$
4 $\times 2$	6 $\times 9$	10 $\times 7$	6 $\times 5$	8 $\times 2$
10 $\times 8$	7 $\times 7$	5 $\times 3$	3 $\times 8$	6 $\times 10$
9 $\times 3$	6 $\times 2$	7 $\times 9$	10 $\times 3$	3 $\times 4$
4 $\times 5$	3 $\times 3$	2 $\times 7$	5 $\times 5$	9 $\times 5$
7 $\times 4$	9 $\times 9$	6 $\times 7$	2 $\times 10$	4 $\times 6$
2 $\times 2$	10 $\times 9$	8 $\times 8$	4 $\times 4$	5 $\times 8$
7 $\times 5$	10 $\times 10$	9 $\times 4$	3 $\times 6$	6 $\times 6$
10 $\times 5$	3 $\times 7$	9 $\times 8$	2 $\times 3$	8 $\times 6$

8V More Facts Practice

Find the number for *n* that will make each number sentence true. Then write the other number sentences in the same fact family.

A. $n \times 7 = 42$

B. $56 \div n = 8$

C. $20 \div n = 5$

D. $9 \times n = 72$

E. $64 \div n = 8$

F. $n \div 4 = 7$

Find the number for *n* that will make each number sentence true.

G. $7 \times n = 2800$

H. $n \times 40 = 2000$

I. $800 \times n = 72,000$

J. $n \times 70 = 350$

TIMS Task

A. $6; 7 \times 6 = 42$
$42 \div 7 = 6$
$42 \div 6 = 7$

B. $7; 56 \div 8 = 7$
$7 \times 8 = 56$
$8 \times 7 = 56$

C. $4; 20 \div 5 = 4$
$4 \times 5 = 20$
$5 \times 4 = 20$

D. $8; 8 \times 9 = 72$
$72 \div 8 = 9$
$72 \div 9 = 8$

E. $8; 8 \times 8 = 64$

F. $28; 28 \div 7 = 4$
$4 \times 7 = 28$
$7 \times 4 = 28$

G. 400

H. 50

I. 90

J. 5

Unit 8: Home Practice

Part 1 Triangle Flash Cards: Reviewing All the Facts

Study for the test on all the multiplication facts. Take home your *Triangle Flash Cards* for the 5s and 10s, 2s and 3s, square numbers, 9s, and the last six facts. Study the facts in small groups, about 8–10 facts each night.

Here's how to use the flash cards. Ask a family member to choose one flash card at a time. Your partner should cover the corner containing the highest number. This number will be the answer to a multiplication fact. Multiply the two uncovered numbers.

Separate the used cards into three piles: those facts you know and can answer quickly, those that you can figure out with a strategy, and those that you need to learn. Practice the last two piles again. Remember to concentrate on one small group of facts each night—about 8 to 10 facts. Also, remember to study only those facts you cannot answer correctly and quickly.

If you do not have your flash cards, create new ones for those facts that are not yet circled on your *Multiplication Facts I Know* chart. To create your flash cards, use the *Triangle Flash Cards Masters* that follow the Home Practice.

Your teacher will tell you when the test on all the multiplication facts will be.

LESSON GUIDE

Facts I Know: Multiplication and Division Facts

Estimated Class Sessions: 1

In Part 1 of this lesson students complete their review of the multiplication facts by taking the *Multiplication Facts Inventory Test.* This appears as DPP Bit U.

Part 2 is a brief exploration and review of fact families. In Part 3, students begin their systematic study and assessment of the division facts using *Triangle Flash Cards* and *Division Facts I Know* charts.

Key Content

- Assessing the multiplication facts.
- Self-assessing the division facts for the 5s and 10s.
- Writing the four related number sentences in a fact family.
- Using known multiplication facts to learn related division facts.

Key Vocabulary

divisor
quotient

Daily Practice and Problems:
Bit for Lesson 8

U. Multiplication Facts
   Inventory Test (URG p. 22)

Students take the *Multiplication Facts Inventory Test.* It contains the multiplication facts from all five groups: 5s and 10s, 2s and 3s, square numbers, 9s, and the last six facts.

We recommend allowing four minutes for this test. Students should have two pens or pencils of different colors ready. During the first four minutes of the test, students write their answers using one color pen or pencil. Encourage students to answer first all the facts they know well and can answer quickly. Then, they should go back and use strategies to solve the rest. After you tell students that four minutes have passed, give them more time to complete the remaining items with the other color pen or pencil.

Students update their *Multiplication Facts I Know* charts using the results of the test.

DPP Task is on page 99. Suggestions for using the DPPs are on page 99.

Curriculum Sequence

Before This Unit

Grade 3 Units 11–20 included systematic practice and assessment of the multiplication facts.

In Grade 4 Unit 3, students began systematically reviewing the multiplication facts and using their knowledge of the multiplication facts to develop strategies for learning the division facts.

After This Unit

In Unit 9, students will use the *Triangle Flash Cards: 5s* and *10s* to practice the division facts. Students will continue practicing the multiplication and division facts in small groups, throughout Units 9–16. In Unit 16, their fluency with the division facts will be assessed with an inventory test. See the Daily Practice and Problems Guide for Unit 9 for information on the distribution of division facts practice and assessment.

Materials List

Print Materials for Students

		Math Facts and Daily Practice and Problems	Assessment Activity	Written Assessment
Student Books	**Student Guide**		*Facts I Know: Multiplication and Division Facts* Pages 234–236	
	Discovery Assignment Book		*Triangle Flash Cards: 5s* Page 115, *Triangle Flash Cards: 10s* Page 117, and *Division Facts I Know* chart Page 119	
Teacher Resources	**Facts Resource Guide** ◎	DPP Items 8U & 8V Use *Triangle Flash Cards: 5s* and *Triangle Flash Cards: 10s* to practice division facts for 5s and 10s.	*Division Facts I Know* chart	DPP Item 8U *Multiplication Facts Inventory Test*
	Unit Resource Guide ◎	DPP Items U–V Pages 22–23		DPP Item U *Multiplication Facts Inventory Test* Pages 22 & 24 ◎
	Generic Section ◎		*Dot Paper, Triangle Flash Cards: 5s,* and *Triangle Flash Cards: 10s,* 1 each per student (optional)	

◎ *available on Teacher Resource CD*

All Transparency Masters, Blackline Masters, and Assessment Blackline Masters in the Unit Resource Guide are on the Teacher Resource CD.

Supplies for Each Student

scissors, optional
ruler, optional
envelope for storing flash cards

Materials for the Teacher

Transparency of *Triangle Flash Cards: 5s* Activity Page (Discovery Assignment Book) Page 115
Transparency of *Triangle Flash Cards: 10s* Activity Page (Discovery Assignment Book) Page 117
Transparency of *Division Facts I Know* Activity Page (Discovery Assignment Book) Page 119
Observational Assessment Record (Unit Resource Guide, Pages 7–8 and Teacher Resource CD)
Individual Assessment Record Sheet (Teacher Implementation Guide, Assessment section and Teacher Resource CD)

Before the Activity

Part 3 of this lesson introduces students to the use of *Triangle Flash Cards* to practice division facts. The *Triangle Flash Cards: 5s* and *10s* are located in the *Discovery Assignment Book* for this lesson. Have students cut out the cards and place them in envelopes.

TIMS Tip

For more durable flash cards, copy the *Triangle Flash Cards* in the Generic Section onto card stock or laminate the cards. You can give students two sets of cards so that they can take a set home and leave a set at school.

Part 1. *Multiplication Facts Inventory Test*

Students take the test as described in DPP Bit U. Allow four minutes for the test. At the end of the four minutes, have students change pencils and finish the test. Students update their *Multiplication Facts I Know* charts.

Have students discuss strategies for any remaining facts that they do not know well and record the strategies in their journals. Students can continue to practice these facts with *Triangle Flash Cards* at home.

Part 2. Picturing Fact Families

Students review fact families through the use of grids (arrays). By this time, most students will be comfortable with fact families and can review this section quickly. For students who are still struggling with the concept, this exercise provides a visual image to help develop their understanding. These students may benefit from drawing the two grids on a piece of centimeter dot paper. Students first examine and draw a grid divided into 20 squares by making 4 rows *(Question 1)*. Next they examine and draw a grid divided into 20 squares by making 5 rows *(Question 2)*. They write the appropriate number sentence on each rectangle they have drawn, using the number of rows as the divisor. Ask students:

- *What multiplication sentence describes each rectangle?*
- *Write that multiplication sentence on the rectangle with the division sentence.*

Have students cut out the rectangles they have drawn on grid paper. By rotating one and placing it on the other, they will see that both grids are the same. All four number sentences ($5 \times 4 = 20$, $4 \times 5 = 20$, $20 \div 5 = 4$, $20 \div 4 = 5$) describe the same rectangle. All are related and belong to the same **fact family.**

Facts I Know: Multiplication and Division Facts

Picturing Fact Families

1. The picture below represents the following problem: If a rectangle has a total of 20 squares in 4 rows, how many squares are in each row?

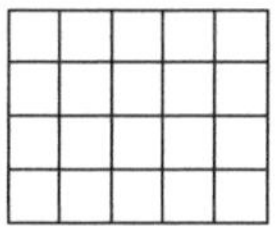

What division sentence describes this problem?

2. The picture below represents the following problem: If a rectangle has a total of 20 squares in 5 rows, how many squares are in each row?

   A. What division sentence describes this problem?
   B. These two division sentences are members of the same **fact family.** What are the other number sentences that are in this same fact family?

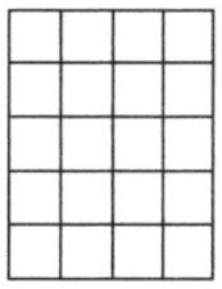

3. Solve the given fact. Then name other facts in the same fact family.
   A. $9 \times 7 = ?$ B. $6 \times 4 = ?$ C. $7 \times 8 = ?$

Division Facts and *Triangle Flash Cards*

4. The directions that follow tell you how to use your *Triangle Flash Cards* to practice the division facts. Work with a partner. Use your *Triangle Flash Cards: 5s* and *10s*.

Student Guide - Page 234

A. One partner covers the number in the square. This number will be the answer to a division problem. The answer to a division problem is called the **quotient.** The number in the circle is the **divisor.** The divisor is the number that divides the largest number on the flash card. The second person solves a division fact with the two uncovered numbers as shown below.

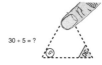

$30 \div 5 = ?$

B. Place each flash card in one of three piles: those facts you know well and can answer quickly, those that you can figure out with a strategy, and those that you need to learn.

C. Begin your *Division Facts I Know* chart. Circle the facts you know well and can answer quickly.

For example, Jacob knew $30 \div 5 = 6$. 5 is the divisor, so Jacob circled the 30 in the row for a divisor of 5.

Division Facts I Know

×	0	1	2	3	4	5	6	7	8	9	10
0	0	0	0	0	0	0	0	0	0	0	0
1	0	1	2	3	4	5	6	7	8	9	10
2	0	2	4	6	8	10	12	14	16	18	20
3	0	3	6	9	12	15	18	21	24	27	30
4	0	4	8	12	16	20	24	28	32	36	40
5	0	5	10	15	20	25	(30)	35	40	45	50
6	0	6	12	18	24	30	36	42	48	54	60
7	0	7	14	21	28	35	42	49	56	63	70
8	0	8	16	24	32	40	48	56	64	72	80
9	0	9	18	27	36	45	54	63	72	81	90
10	0	10	20	30	40	50	60	70	80	90	100

Divisor (label on left side)

Recording $30 \div 5 = 6$ as a Fact I Know.

Student Guide - Page 235

D. Sort the 5s and 10s flashcards again. This time your partner covers the number in the circle. The number in the square is now the **divisor** and the covered number in the circle is the answer to the division problem, the **quotient**. If we use the same example, 6 is now the **divisor**. Jacob knew this division problem also, 30 ÷ 6 = 5, so he drew a circle around the 30 in the row for a divisor of 6 on his *Division Facts I Know* chart. He circled 30 twice on his chart.

30 ÷ 6 = ?

E. Update your *Division Facts I Know* chart each time you go through the set of *Triangle Flash Cards*. Circle the facts you know well and can answer quickly.

F. Discuss how you can figure out facts you do not recall right away. Share your strategies with your partner.

G. Practice the last two piles at home for homework—the facts you can figure out with a strategy and those you need to learn. Make a list of these facts.

5. As you practice the division facts and update your *Division Facts I Know* chart, compare it to your *Multiplication Facts I Know* chart. Look for facts in the same fact family. Do you know any complete fact families? Which family or families? Explain.

You will continue to use *Triangle Flash Cards* to study all the groups of division facts in the units to come. You will update your *Division Facts I Know* chart each time you go through the cards. If you know one or two of the facts in a fact family, use those facts to help you learn the others.

236 SG · Grade 4 · Unit 8 · Lesson 8   Facts I Know

Division Facts I Know

×	0	1	2	3	4	5	6	7	8	9	10
0	0	0	0	0	0	0	0	0	0	0	0
1	0	1	2	3	4	5	6	7	8	9	10
2	0	2	4	6	8	10	12	14	16	18	20
3	0	3	6	9	12	15	18	21	24	27	30
4	0	4	8	12	16	20	24	28	32	36	40
5	0	5	10	15	20	25	(30)	35	40	45	50
6	0	6	12	18	24	30	36	42	48	54	60
7	0	7	14	21	28	35	42	49	56	63	70
8	0	8	16	24	32	40	48	56	64	72	80
9	0	9	18	27	36	45	54	63	72	81	90
10	0	10	20	30	40	50	60	70	80	90	100

Divisor (row label)

Recording 30 ÷ 5 = 6 as a Fact I Know.

Figure 16: *Using the* Division Facts I Know *chart*

Part 3. Division Facts and Triangle Flash Cards

Have student pairs use their *Triangle Flash Cards: 5s* and their *Triangle Flash Cards: 10s* to begin assessing their progress with learning the division facts.

Question 4 in the *Student Guide* outlines using the flash cards for division. As partners quiz each other on the facts, students sort the cards into three piles—those they know and can answer quickly, those facts they know using a strategy, and those facts they need to learn. The procedure here is similar to the way the cards were used earlier for multiplication. There is one main difference, however. When using the cards for division, students need to sort the *Triangle Flash Cards* twice. The first time through the set of cards, partners cover the numbers in squares *(Question 4A–4B)*.

Then, after the cards are sorted, students begin their *Division Facts I Know* charts *(Question 4C)*. The second time through, partners cover the numbers in circles *(Question 4D)*. After the entire set of cards is sorted for the second time, the students update their division charts *(Question 4E)*. See Figure 15. Demonstrate this sequence using transparencies of the flash cards and the *Division Facts I Know* chart.

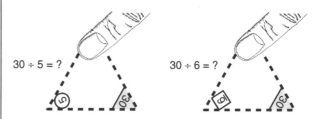

30 ÷ 5 = ?   30 ÷ 6 = ?

Figure 15: *Sort the cards twice—once covering the numbers in squares and a second time covering the numbers in circles.*

Question 4C provides an example of how to use the *Division Facts I Know* chart. Turn students' attention to the chart shown in the *Student Guide*. Since Jacob divided by 5 (30 ÷ 5 = 6), 5 is the **divisor.** He followed the 5 across its row to find the 30 he should circle. See Figure 16. Remind students that they circle only those facts that were in the pile of facts they know and can answer quickly. They make a list of the facts in the other two piles and take this list home along with their flash cards so they can study the facts with a family member.

Question 5 asks students to compare their *Multiplication Facts I Know* charts with their *Division Facts I Know* charts. If students are using their knowledge of the multiplication facts and fact families to help them learn the division facts, they will see some patterns in their charts. For example, if a student knows 4 × 5 and 5 × 4, it is very likely he or she will know 20 ÷ 4 and 20 ÷ 5. Thus, two 20s should be circled on the division chart as well. Note that both *Facts I Know* charts have a multiplication symbol in the first square since both charts are simply multiplication tables used for recording known facts.

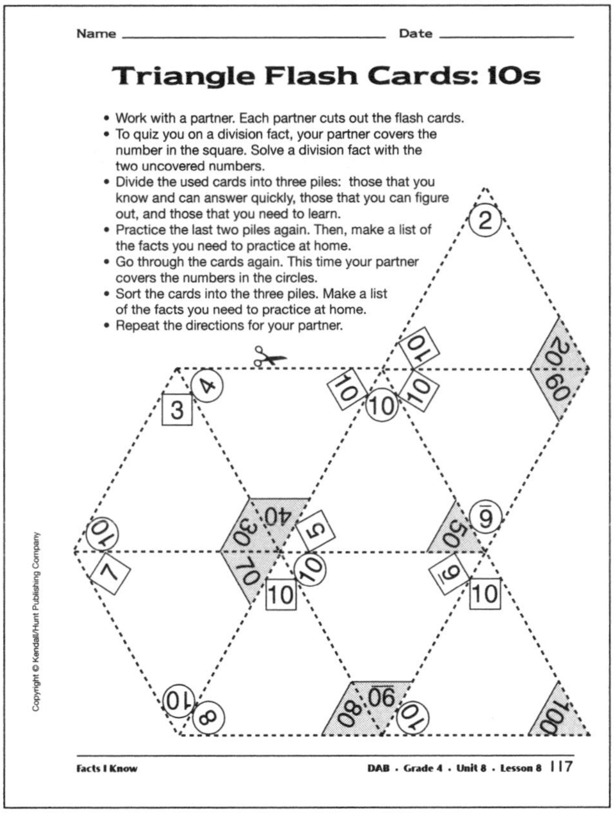

Name ______________ Date ______________

Triangle Flash Cards: 10s

- Work with a partner. Each partner cuts out the flash cards.
- To quiz you on a division fact, your partner covers the number in the square. Solve a division fact with the two uncovered numbers.
- Divide the used cards into three piles: those that you know and can answer quickly, those that you can figure out, and those that you need to learn.
- Practice the last two piles again. Then, make a list of the facts you need to practice at home.
- Go through the cards again. This time your partner covers the numbers in the circles.
- Sort the cards into the three piles. Make a list of the facts you need to practice at home.
- Repeat the directions for your partner.

Copyright © Kendall/Hunt Publishing Company

Facts I Know DAB • Grade 4 • Unit 8 • Lesson 8 117

***Discovery Assignment Book* - Page 117**

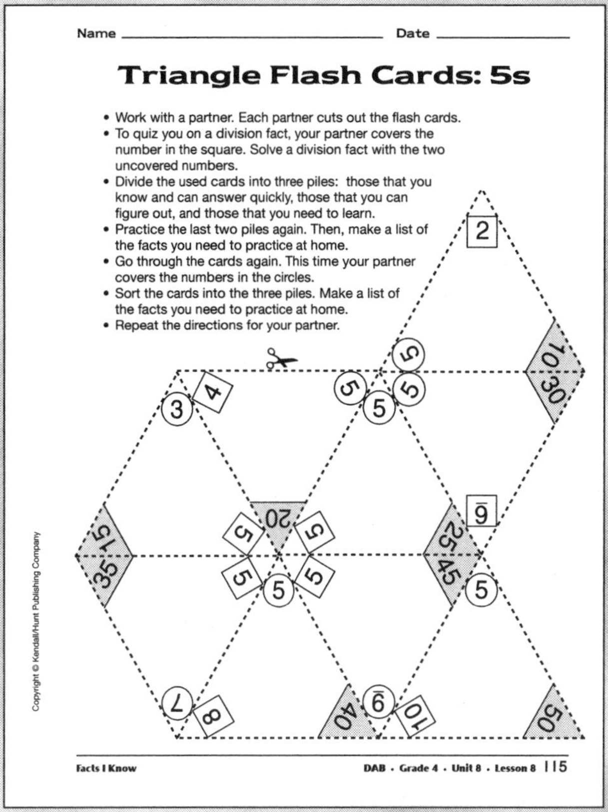

Name ______________ Date ______________

Triangle Flash Cards: 5s

- Work with a partner. Each partner cuts out the flash cards.
- To quiz you on a division fact, your partner covers the number in the square. Solve a division fact with the two uncovered numbers.
- Divide the used cards into three piles: those that you know and can answer quickly, those that you can figure out, and those that you need to learn.
- Practice the last two piles again. Then, make a list of the facts you need to practice at home.
- Go through the cards again. This time your partner covers the numbers in the circles.
- Sort the cards into the three piles. Make a list of the facts you need to practice at home.
- Repeat the directions for your partner.

Copyright © Kendall/Hunt Publishing Company

Facts I Know DAB • Grade 4 • Unit 8 • Lesson 8 115

***Discovery Assignment Book* - Page 115**

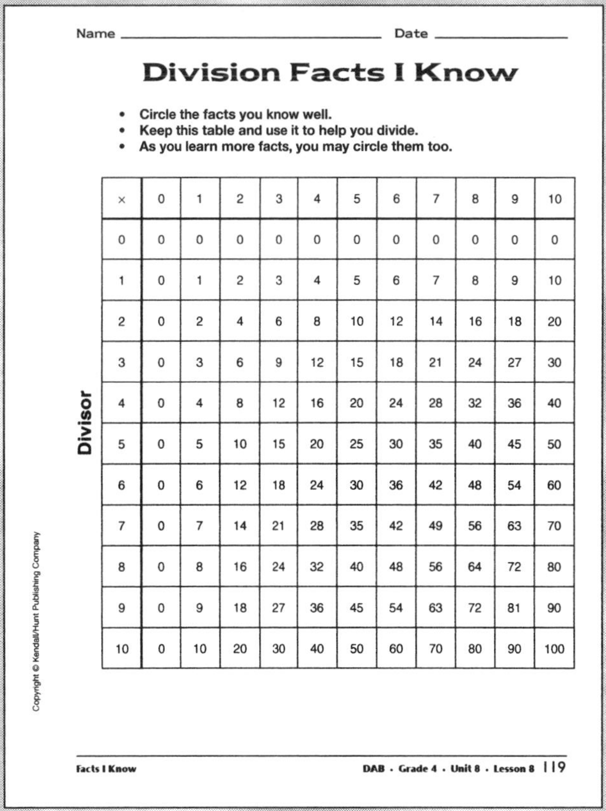

Name ______________ Date ______________

Division Facts I Know

- **Circle the facts you know well.**
- **Keep this table and use it to help you divide.**
- **As you learn more facts, you may circle them too.**

Divisor

×	0	1	2	3	4	5	6	7	8	9	10
0	0	0	0	0	0	0	0	0	0	0	0
1	0	1	2	3	4	5	6	7	8	9	10
2	0	2	4	6	8	10	12	14	16	18	20
3	0	3	6	9	12	15	18	21	24	27	30
4	0	4	8	12	16	20	24	28	32	36	40
5	0	5	10	15	20	25	30	35	40	45	50
6	0	6	12	18	24	30	36	42	48	54	60
7	0	7	14	21	28	35	42	49	56	63	70
8	0	8	16	24	32	40	48	56	64	72	80
9	0	9	18	27	36	45	54	63	72	81	90
10	0	10	20	30	40	50	60	70	80	90	100

Copyright © Kendall/Hunt Publishing Company

Facts I Know DAB • Grade 4 • Unit 8 • Lesson 8 119

***Discovery Assignment Book* - Page 119**

Daily Practice and Problems: Task for Lesson 8

V. Task: More Facts Practice

(URG p. 23)

Find the number for *n* that will make each number sentence true. Then write the other number sentences in the same fact family.

A. $n \times 7 = 42$

B. $56 \div n = 8$

C. $20 \div n = 5$

D. $9 \times n = 72$

E. $64 \div n = 8$

F. $n \div 4 = 7$

Find the number for *n* that will make each number sentence true.

G. $7 \times n = 2800$

H. $n \times 40 = 2000$

I. $800 \times n = 72,000$

J. $n \times 70 = 350$

Suggestions for Teaching the Lesson

Math Facts

DPP Task V provides practice with using multiplication facts to complete number sentences and to multiply numbers that end in zero. It also provides practice with division facts.

Assessment

- DPP Bit U is the *Multiplication Facts Inventory Test*. Have students change pens or pencils after four minutes. Record students' progress with the multiplication facts on the *Observational Assessment Record*.

- Transfer appropriate documentation from the Unit 8 *Observational Assessment Record* to students' *Individual Assessment Record Sheets*.

AT A GLANCE

Math Facts and Daily Practice and Problems

DPP Bit U is the *Multiplication Facts Inventory Test.* Task V provides practice with multiplication and division facts.

Part 1. *Multiplication Facts Inventory Test*

Students take the *Multiplication Facts Inventory Test* in DPP item U. Allow four minutes for the test. Then let students change to a different pen and finish the test. Students update their *Multiplication Facts I Know* charts.

Part 2. Picturing Fact Families

1. Students read and discuss the Picturing Fact Families section in the *Student Guide.*
2. Students draw and cut out two 5×4 rectangles on dot paper. (optional)
3. Students list the four fact families that describe a 5×4 rectangle.

Part 3. Division Facts and Triangle Flash Cards

1. Students read the Division Facts and *Triangle Flash Cards* section in the *Student Guide.*
2. Discuss with the students how to use the *Triangle Flash Cards* to practice division facts, by first covering the numbers in the squares and then covering the numbers in the circles.
3. Show the transparency of a *Division Facts I Know* chart.
4. Model marking a *Division Facts I Know* chart with a sample division fact.

Assessment

1. Use the *Multiplication Facts Inventory Test* in DPP Bit U and the *Observational Assessment Record* to document students' fluency with the multiplication facts.
2. Transfer appropriate documentation from the Unit 8 *Observational Assessment Record* to the students' *Individual Assessment Record Sheets.*

Notes:

Answer Key • Lesson 8: Facts I Know: Multiplication and Division Facts

Student Guide

Questions 1–5 (SG pp. 234–236)

1. $20 \div 4 = 5$
2. **A.** $20 \div 5 = 4$
   B. $4 \times 5 = 20; 5 \times 4 = 20$

3. **A.** $63; 7 \times 9 = 63; 63 \div 7 = 9; 63 \div 9 = 7$
   B. $24; 4 \times 6 = 24; 24 \div 4 = 6; 24 \div 6 = 4$
   C. $56; 8 \times 7 = 56; 56 \div 8 = 7; 56 \div 7 = 8$
4.–5. *

*Answers and/or discussion are included in the Lesson Guide.
**Answers for all the Home Practice in the *Discovery Assignment Book* are at the end of the unit.

Facts I Know: Multiplication and Division Facts

Picturing Fact Families

1. The picture below represents the following problem: If a rectangle has a total of 20 squares in 4 rows, how many squares are in each row?

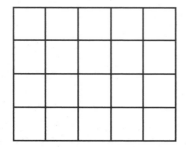

   What division sentence describes this problem?

2. The picture below represents the following problem: If a rectangle has a total of 20 squares in 5 rows, how many squares are in each row?

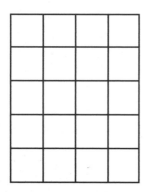

   A. What division sentence describes this problem?

   B. These two division sentences are members of the same **fact family.** What are the other number sentences that are in this same fact family?

3. Solve the given fact. Then name other facts in the same fact family.

   A. $9 \times 7 = ?$ **B.** $6 \times 4 = ?$ **C.** $7 \times 8 = ?$

Division Facts and *Triangle Flash Cards*

4. The directions that follow tell you how to use your *Triangle Flash Cards* to practice the division facts. Work with a partner. Use your *Triangle Flash Cards: 5s* and *10s*.

A. One partner covers the number in the square. This number will be the answer to a division problem. The answer to a division problem is called the **quotient.** The number in the circle is the **divisor.** The divisor is the number that divides the largest number on the flash card. The second person solves a division fact with the two uncovered numbers as shown below.

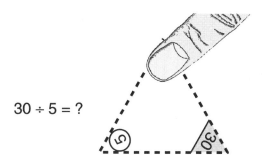

$30 \div 5 = ?$

B. Place each flash card in one of three piles: those facts you know well and can answer quickly, those that you can figure out with a strategy, and those that you need to learn.

C. Begin your *Division Facts I Know* chart. Circle the facts you know well and can answer quickly.

For example, Jacob knew $30 \div 5 = 6$. 5 is the divisor, so Jacob circled the 30 in the row for a divisor of 5.

Division Facts I Know

×	0	1	2	3	4	5	6	7	8	9	10
0	0	0	0	0	0	0	0	0	0	0	0
1	0	1	2	3	4	5	6	7	8	9	10
2	0	2	4	6	8	10	12	14	16	18	20
3	0	3	6	9	12	15	18	21	24	27	30
4	0	4	8	12	16	20	24	28	32	36	40
5	0	5	10	15	20	25	(30)	35	40	45	50
6	0	6	12	18	24	30	36	42	48	54	60
7	0	7	14	21	28	35	42	49	56	63	70
8	0	8	16	24	32	40	48	56	64	72	80
9	0	9	18	27	36	45	54	63	72	81	90
10	0	10	20	30	40	50	60	70	80	90	100

Divisor

Recording $30 \div 5 = 6$ as a Fact I Know.

D. Sort the 5s and 10s flashcards again. This time your partner covers the number in the circle. The number in the square is now the **divisor** and the covered number in the circle is the answer to the division problem, the **quotient.** If we use the same example, 6 is now the **divisor.** Jacob knew this division problem also, 30 ÷ 6 = 5, so he drew a circle around the 30 in the row for a divisor of 6 on his *Division Facts I Know* chart. He circled 30 twice on his chart.

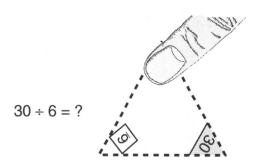

30 ÷ 6 = ?

E. Update your *Division Facts I Know* chart each time you go through the set of *Triangle Flash Cards.* Circle the facts you know well and can answer quickly.

F. Discuss how you can figure out facts you do not recall right away. Share your strategies with your partner.

G. Practice the last two piles at home for homework—the facts you can figure out with a strategy and those you need to learn. Make a list of these facts.

5. As you practice the division facts and update your *Division Facts I Know* chart, compare it to your *Multiplication Facts I Know* chart. Look for facts in the same fact family. Do you know any complete fact families? Which family or families? Explain.

You will continue to use *Triangle Flash Cards* to study all the groups of division facts in the units to come. You will update your *Division Facts I Know* chart each time you go through the cards. If you know one or two of the facts in a fact family, use those facts to help you learn the others.

Name _____ Date _____

Division Facts I Know

- Circle the facts you know well.
- Keep this table and use it to help you divide.
- As you learn more facts, you may circle them too.

Divisor

×	0	1	2	3	4	5	6	7	8	9	10
0	0	0	0	0	0	0	0	0	0	0	0
1	0	1	2	3	4	5	6	7	8	9	10
2	0	2	4	6	8	10	12	14	16	18	20
3	0	3	6	9	12	15	18	21	24	27	30
4	0	4	8	12	16	20	24	28	32	36	40
5	0	5	10	15	20	25	30	35	40	45	50
6	0	6	12	18	24	30	36	42	48	54	60
7	0	7	14	21	28	35	42	49	56	63	70
8	0	8	16	24	32	40	48	56	64	72	80
9	0	9	18	27	36	45	54	63	72	81	90
10	0	10	20	30	40	50	60	70	80	90	100

Facts Distribution
Division:
5s and 10s · Weeks 21-22

Math Facts Groups	Weeks	Daily Practice and Problems	Home Practice	Triangle Flash Cards	Facts Quizzes and Tests
Division Practice for the 5s and 10s	21–22	Unit 9: Items 9B, 9C, 9E, 9K, 9M, 9O, 9R, 9U & 9V	Unit 9 Parts 1 & 2	*Triangle Flash Cards: 5s and 10s*	DPP Item 9U is a quiz on the division facts for the 5s and 10s. The *Division Facts I Know* chart is updated.

Students may solve the items individually, in groups, or as a class. The items may also be assigned for homework.

Student Questions	Teacher Notes

 Fact Families for × and ÷

The following four facts are in the same fact family:

$7 \times 10 = 70$ $10 \times 7 = 70$

$70 \div 7 = 10$ $70 \div 10 = 7$

Solve each pair of related number sentences.

Then, give two other facts that are in the same fact family.

A. $5 \times 4 = ?$ and $20 \div 4 = ?$

B. $3 \times 10 = ?$ and $30 \div 3 = ?$

C. $10 \times 5 = ?$ and $50 \div 10 = ?$

D. $8 \times 5 = ?$ and $40 \div 5 = ?$

E. $6 \times 10 = ?$ and $60 \div 6 = ?$

F. $10 \times 8 = ?$ and $80 \div 8 = ?$

TIMS Task

A. 20; 5; $4 \times 5 = 20$;
   $20 \div 5 = 4$

B. 30; 10; $10 \times 3 = 30$;
   $30 \div 10 = 3$

C. 50; 5; $5 \times 10 = 50$;
   $50 \div 5 = 10$

D. 40; 8; $5 \times 8 = 40$;
   $40 \div 8 = 5$

E. 60; 10; $10 \times 6 = 60$;
   $60 \div 10 = 6$

F. 80; 10; $8 \times 10 = 80$;
   $80 \div 10 = 8$

Student Questions	Teacher Notes

9C Practicing the Facts

TIMS Bit

A. $5 \div 1 =$ B. $40 \div 4 =$

C. $15 \div 3 =$ D. $100 \div 10 =$

E. $45 \div 5 =$ F. $25 \div 5 =$

G. $60 \div 10 =$ H. $35 \div 7 =$

I. $10 \div 5 =$ J. $30 \div 5 =$

K. $0 \div 5 =$

A. 5
B. 10
C. 5
D. 10
E. 9
F. 5
G. 6
H. 5
I. 2
J. 6
K. 0

9E Division Stories

TIMS Bit

The following two problems can be solved using division.

Pictures will vary, but the important idea here is that division is used to sort and organize larger numbers into smaller, even groups of numbers.

1. Mrs. Randall gave each of her children $4 to spend on games at the neighborhood carnival. If Mrs. Randall gave out $20 in all, how many children does she have? Draw a picture to show this problem.

   1. $20 in all $\div$ $4 to each child = 5 children

2. One package of bus tokens contains 10 tokens. Keenya's mother needs 40 tokens to get to and from work for one month. How many packages does Keenya's mother need? Draw a picture to show this problem.

   2. 40 tokens $\div$ 10 tokens per package = 4 packages

9K **More Fact Practice**

Find *n* to make each number sentence true.

A. $8 \times 5 = n$ B. $n \times 7 = 70$

C. $n \div 4 = 5$ D. $80 \div n = 10$

E. $10 \times n = 50$ F. $30 \div 5 = n$

G. $9 \times 10 = n$ H. $15 \div n = 5$

I. $n \times 8 = 80$ J. $10 \div 10 = n$

TIMS Bit

A. 40	B. 10
C. 20	D. 8
E. 5	F. 6
G. 90	H. 3
I. 10	J. 1

9M **More Fact Families for × and ÷**

New uniforms for the cheerleading and pompom squads were delivered today at Oakland High. Each box contained 8 uniforms. If 40 uniforms were ordered in all, how many boxes arrived?

There are 5 groups of 8 in 40. Think: $? \times 8 = 40$ or $40 \div 8 = ?$

The answer to both questions is 5.

Solve the following problems. Each group of facts is related.

A. $10 \times 7 =$ $70 \div 7 =$

  $7 \times 10 =$ $70 \div 10 =$

B. $2 \times 5 =$ $10 \div 5 =$

  $5 \times 2 =$ $10 \div 2 =$

C. $6 \times 5 =$ $30 \div 5 =$

  $5 \times 6 =$ $30 \div 6 =$

TIMS Bit

Among other strategies, students can use their knowledge of the multiplication facts to solve division facts. Encourage students to share their strategies.

A. 70; 10; 70; 7

B. 10; 2; 10; 5

C. 30; 6; 30; 5

9O Multiplying by Multiples of Ten

A. $8 \times 500 =$ B. $6 \times 100 =$

C. $2 \times 5000 =$ D. $5000 \times 6 =$

E. $50,000 \times 1 =$ F. $9 \times 50 =$

TIMS Bit

A. 4000

B. 600

C. 10,000

D. 30,000

E. 50,000

F. 450

9R Even More Fact Families for × and ÷

The following four facts are in the same fact family:

$6 \times 5 = 30$ $5 \times 6 = 30$

$30 \div 5 = 6$ $30 \div 6 = 5$

Solve each pair of related number sentences.

Then, give two other facts that are in the same fact family.

A. $2 \times 10 = ?$ and $20 \div 10 = ?$

B. $3 \times 5 = ?$ and $15 \div 5 = ?$

C. $7 \times 5 = ?$ and $35 \div 7 = ?$

D. $10 \times 9 = ?$ and $90 \div 9 = ?$

E. $4 \times 10 = ?$ and $40 \div 10 = ?$

F. $5 \times 9 = ?$ and $45 \div 9 = ?$

TIMS Task

A. 20; 2; $10 \times 2 = 20$ and $20 \div 2 = 10$

B. 15; 3; $5 \times 3 = 15$ and $15 \div 3 = 5$

C. 35; 5; $5 \times 7 = 35$ and $35 \div 5 = 7$

D. 90; 10; $9 \times 10 = 90$ and $90 \div 10 = 9$

E. 40; 4; $10 \times 4 = 40$ and $40 \div 4 = 10$

F. 45; 5; $9 \times 5 = 45$ and $45 \div 5 = 9$

Student Questions	Teacher Notes

9U Quiz: 5s and 10s

A. 30 ÷ 3 =

B. 10 ÷ 1 =

C. 10 ÷ 2 =

D. 60 ÷ 10 =

E. 40 ÷ 8 =

F. 5 ÷ 5 =

G. 20 ÷ 5 =

H. 80 ÷ 10 =

I. 30 ÷ 6 =

J. 35 ÷ 5 =

K. 15 ÷ 3 =

L. 50 ÷ 10 =

M. 70 ÷ 10 =

N. 90 ÷ 9 =

O. 40 ÷ 4 =

P. 20 ÷ 2 =

Q. 100 ÷ 10 =

R. 25 ÷ 5 =

S. 45 ÷ 5 =

TIMS Bit

We recommend 2 minutes for this quiz. Allow students to change pens after the time is up and complete the remaining problems in a different color. After students take the test, have them update their *Division Facts I Know* charts.

It is likely that a student who answers 40 ÷ 8 correctly also knows the answer to 40 ÷ 5. To make sure, after the quiz, ask students to write a related division fact, if possible. The square numbers only have one division sentence (e.g., 25 ÷ 5 = 5). Then, students who answer a fact correctly and who also write the correct related fact, can circle both facts on the chart.

9V Who Am I?

Answer each riddle below.

1. I am three less than five squared.

2. I am two times as great as the sum of five and eight.

3. I am half the difference of ten and four.

4. I am six more than the product of nine and three.

5. If you subtract the product of four and three from the sum of eleven and four, you will know who I am.

6. Make up your own riddle to share.

TIMS Challenge

1. 25 − 3 = 22

2. 13 × 2 = 26

3. 6 ÷ 2 = 3

4. 27 + 6 = 33

5. 15 − 12 = 3

6. Answers will vary.

Unit 9: Home Practice

Part 1 Triangle Flash Cards: 5s and 10s

Study for the quiz on the multiplication facts for the 5s and 10s. Take home your *Triangle Flash Cards* and your list of facts you need to study.

Here's how to use the flash cards. Ask a family member to choose one flash card at a time. Your partner should cover one of the smaller numbers. (One of the smaller numbers is in a circle. The other number is in a square.) Solve a division fact using the two uncovered numbers. Go through the cards a second time, this time cover the other small number.

Your teacher will tell you when the quiz on the 5s and 10s will be. Remember to concentrate on one small group of facts each night—about 8 to 10 facts. Also, remember to concentrate on those facts you cannot answer correctly and quickly.

Part 2 Mental Multiplication

1. Use mental math to solve Questions 1A–1F.

   A. $6000 \times 10 =$ _____   B. $500 \times 70 =$ _____

   C. $60 \times 60 =$ _____   D. $9000 \times 5 =$ _____

   E. $100 \times 800 =$ _____   F. $500 \times 50 =$ _____

2. A. Paper towels cost 80¢. How much will 6 rolls cost?

   B. One ice cream bar costs $3.50. How much will 4 bars cost?

   C. Bagels cost 69¢ each. About how much will 5 bagels cost?

3. How much is:
   A. 13 nickels?

   B. 11 nickels and 5 dimes?

   C. 5 quarters and 17 nickels?

Section 5

Facts Distribution
Division:
2s and 3s · Weeks 23-24

Division Practice
for the
2s and 3s

Math Facts Groups	Weeks	Daily Practice and Problems	Home Practice	Triangle Flash Cards	Facts Quizzes and Tests
Division Practice for the 2s and 3s	23–24	Unit 10: Items 10B–10D, 10G, 10K, 10M, 10Q, 10W & 10X	Unit 10 Part 1	*Triangle Flash Cards: 2s and 3s*	DPP Item 10W is a quiz on the division facts for the 2s and 3s. The *Division Facts I Know* chart is updated.

Daily Practice and Problems

Students may solve the items individually, in groups, or as a class. The items may also be assigned for homework.

Student Questions	Teacher Notes

 Triangle Flash Cards: 2s and 3s

With a partner, use your *Triangle Flash Cards* to quiz each other on the division facts for the twos and threes. One partner covers the corner containing the number in a circle. This covered number will be the answer to a division fact, called the quotient. The number in the square is the divisor. Use the two uncovered numbers to solve a division fact.

Separate the used cards into three piles: those facts you know and can answer quickly, those that you can figure out with a strategy, and those that you need to learn. Make a list of those facts that are in the last two piles.

Put the cards back into one pile and go through them a second time with your partner. This time, your partner covers the number in the square. This number will now be the quotient. The number in the circle is now the divisor. Use the two uncovered numbers to solve a division fact.

Separate the cards again into three piles. Add the facts in the last two piles to your list. Take the list home to practice.

Circle the facts you know quickly on your *Division Facts I Know* chart.

TIMS Task

The *Triangle Flash Cards: 2s and 3s* are located in the *Discovery Assignment Book* after the Home Practice.

Blackline masters of the flash cards can be found in the *Unit Resource Guide* Generic Section. After students sort the cards, encourage them to practice the facts in the last two piles. As the class discusses strategies, emphasize those strategies that are more efficient than others. (See DPP items C and G.)

The Home Practice reminds students to bring home their *Triangle Flash Cards* for the 2s and 3s, and to study only small groups of facts (8–10 facts) at one time.

Inform students when the quiz on the 2s and 3s will be given. This quiz appears in item W.

10C **Fact Families for × and ÷**

The following four facts belong to the same fact family.

$3 \times 2 = 6$ $2 \times 3 = 6$

$6 \div 2 = 3$ $6 \div 3 = 2$

Solve each pair of related number sentences.

Then, give two other facts that are in the same fact family.

A. $3 \times 9 = ?$ and $27 \div 9 = ?$

B. $2 \times 10 = ?$ and $20 \div 10 = ?$

C. $2 \times 8 = ?$ and $16 \div 2 = ?$

D. $6 \times 2 = ?$ and $12 \div 6 = ?$

E. $10 \times 3 = ?$ and $30 \div 3 = ?$

F. $5 \times 2 = ?$ and $10 \div 5 = ?$

G. $1 \times 2 = ?$ and $2 \div 2 = ?$

Complete this item orally as a class. One student can solve the given facts and two other students can name each of the other two related facts.

A. 27; 3; $9 \times 3 = 27$;
    $27 \div 3 = 9$

B. 20; 2; $10 \times 2 = 20$;
    $20 \div 2 = 10$

C. 16; 8; $8 \times 2 = 16$;
    $16 \div 8 = 2$

D. 12; 2; $2 \times 6 = 12$;
    $12 \div 2 = 6$

E. 30; 10; $3 \times 10 = 30$;
    $30 \div 10 = 3$

F. 10; 2; $2 \times 5 = 10$;
    $10 \div 2 = 5$

G. 2; 1; $2 \times 1 = 2$;
    $2 \div 1 = 2$

10D Base-Ten Shorthand

Write the following numbers or answers in base-ten shorthand. Use the Fewest Pieces Rule.

A bit is one whole.

A. 777

B. 4096

C. 2735

D. 20 × 2

E. 400 × 3

F. 30 × 3

G. 20 × 90

H. 600 × 3

TIMS Task

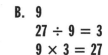

A.

B.

C.

D. /|||

E.

F. /|\|| /|\|

G.

H.

10G Math Fact Practice

Solve the problem. Then write the other number sentences in the same fact family.

A. 15 ÷ 5 =

B. 27 ÷ 3 =

C. 16 ÷ 2 =

D. 18 ÷ 2 =

E. 21 ÷ 3 =

F. 24 ÷ 3 =

G. 2 ÷ 2 =

TIMS Bit

A. 3
  15 ÷ 3 = 5
  5 × 3 = 15
  3 × 5 = 15

B. 9
  27 ÷ 9 = 3
  9 × 3 = 27
  3 × 9 = 27

C. 8
  16 ÷ 8 = 2
  8 × 2 = 16
  2 × 8 = 16

D. 9
  18 ÷ 9 = 2
  9 × 2 = 18
  2 × 9 = 18

E. 7
  21 ÷ 7 = 3
  7 × 3 = 21
  3 × 7 = 21

F. 8
  24 ÷ 8 = 3
  8 × 3 = 24
  3 × 8 = 24

G. 1
  2 ÷ 1 = 2
  2 × 1 = 2
  1 × 2 = 2

10K The Price Is Right

Fill in the table. Find the largest second factor so that the product of the two numbers is close to the target number without going over the target number. The first has been filled in for you.

Factor 1	Factor 2	Target Number	Left Over
5	7	38	3
3		28	
2		17	
7		25	
6		20	
9		48	
4		13	
5		12	

TIMS Bit

Students find the largest one-digit number that will provide a product that does not go over the target number. Students practice division facts by solving problems in which the division does not come out evenly.

Factor 1	Factor 2	Target Number	Left Over
5	7	38	3
3	9	28	1
2	8	17	1
7	3	25	4
6	3	20	2
9	5	48	3
4	3	13	1
5	2	12	2

10M Multiplying with Zeros

A. $80 \times 20 =$ B. $40 \times 3 =$

C. $3000 \times 40 =$ D. $20 \times 500 =$

E. $50 \times 30 =$ F. $600 \times 2 =$

G. $0 \times 20 =$ H. $10 \times 30 =$

TIMS Bit

A. 1600

B. 120

C. 120,000

D. 10,000

E. 1500

F. 1200

G. 0

H. 300

10Q More Fact Families for × and ÷

TIMS Bit

The following four facts are in the same fact family.

$4 \times 3 = 12$ $3 \times 4 = 12$

$12 \div 3 = 4$ $12 \div 4 = 3$

Solve each pair of related number sentences. Then, give two other facts that are in the same fact family.

A. $7 \times 2 = ?$ and $14 \div 7 = ?$

B. $2 \times 3 = ?$ and $6 \div 2 = ?$

C. $3 \times 8 = ?$ and $24 \div 3 = ?$

D. $6 \times 3 = ?$ and $18 \div 3 = ?$

E. $4 \times 2 = ?$ and $8 \div 4 = ?$

F. $3 \times 8 = ?$ and $24 \div 8 = ?$

G. $3 \times 1 = ?$ and $3 \div 1 = ?$

A. 14; 2; $2 \times 7 = 14$; $14 \div 2 = 7$

B. 6; 3; $3 \times 2 = 6$; $6 \div 3 = 2$

C. 24; 8; $8 \times 3 = 24$; $24 \div 8 = 3$

D. 18; 6; $3 \times 6 = 18$; $18 \div 6 = 3$

E. 8; 2; $2 \times 4 = 8$; $8 \div 2 = 4$

F. 24; 3; $8 \times 3 = 24$; $24 \div 3 = 8$

G. 3; 3; $1 \times 3 = 3$; $3 \div 3 = 1$

Student Questions	Teacher Notes

10W Quiz on 2s and 3s Division Facts

A. $8 \div 2 =$
B. $30 \div 3 =$
C. $16 \div 2 =$
D. $9 \div 3 =$
E. $12 \div 2 =$
F. $21 \div 3 =$
G. $15 \div 3 =$
H. $4 \div 2 =$
I. $10 \div 2 =$
J. $27 \div 3 =$
K. $14 \div 2 =$
L. $12 \div 3 =$
M. $6 \div 3 =$
N. $24 \div 3 =$
O. $2 \div 1 =$
P. $18 \div 3 =$
Q. $18 \div 2 =$
R. $3 \div 3 =$
S. $20 \div 2 =$

TIMS Bit

We recommend 2 minutes for this quiz. Allow students to change pens after the time is up and complete the remaining problems in a different color.

After students take the quiz, have them update their *Division Facts I Know* charts. Since students learned the division facts through work with fact families, it is likely that the student who answers $12 \div 2$ correctly also knows the answer to $12 \div 6$. To make sure, however, ask students to write a related division fact for each of the facts on the quiz (except $9 \div 3$ and $4 \div 2$). A student who answers a given fact correctly and who also writes the correct related fact can circle both facts on the chart.

A. 4	B. 10
C. 8	D. 3
E. 6	F. 7
G. 5	H. 2
I. 5	J. 9
K. 7	L. 4
M. 2	N. 8
O. 2	P. 6
Q. 9	R. 1
S. 10	

10X Dividing It Up

$26 \div 8 = ?$ Write a story for $26 \div 8$. Then, draw a picture. Include any remainder in your picture.

TIMS Task

3 R2

Unit 10: Home Practice

Part 1   *Triangle Flash Cards: 2s and 3s*

Study for the quiz on the multiplication facts for the 2s and 3s. Take home your *Triangle Flash Cards* and your list of facts you need to study.

Here's how to use the flash cards. Ask a family member to choose one flash card at a time. Your partner should cover the corner containing either the square or the circle. This number will be the answer to a division fact. Solve a division problem with the two uncovered numbers.

Your teacher will tell you when the quiz on the 2s and 3s will be. Remember to concentrate on one small group of facts each night—about 8 to 10 facts. Also, remember to study only those facts you cannot answer correctly and quickly.

Facts Distribution
Division:
Square Numbers · Weeks 25-26

Math Facts Groups	Weeks	Daily Practice and Problems	Home Practice	Triangle Flash Cards	Facts Quizzes and Tests
Division Practice for the Square Numbers	25–26	Unit 11: Items 11A, 11C, 11E, 11G, 11I, 11Q, 11T & 11U	Unit 11 Parts 1 & 3	*Triangle Flash Cards: Square Numbers*	DPP Item 11U is a quiz on the division facts for the Square Numbers. The *Division Facts I Know* chart is updated.

Students may solve the items individually, in groups, or as a class. The items may also be assigned for homework.

Student Questions	Teacher Notes

 Triangle Flash Cards: Square Numbers

With a partner, use your *Triangle Flash Cards* to quiz each other on the division facts for the square numbers (e.g., 4 ÷ 2 = 2 and 9 ÷ 3 = 3). The highest number on each card is lightly shaded. One partner covers one of the other two corners with his or her thumb. This number will be the answer to a division fact or the quotient. The second person solves a division problem with the other two numbers.

Separate the used cards into three piles: those facts you know and can answer quickly, those that you can figure out with a strategy, and those that you need to learn. Practice the last two piles again and then make a list of the facts you need to practice at home for homework.

Circle the facts you know and can answer quickly on your *Division Facts I Know* chart.

TIMS Bit

The flash cards for the square numbers facts can be found in the *Discovery Assignment Book* following the Home Practice and the *Unit Resource Guide* Generic Section. After students sort the cards, encourage them to practice the facts in the last two piles—those facts that they can figure out with a strategy and those they need to learn. Discuss strategies students use to find the answers to the facts, emphasizing those strategies that are more efficient than others.

Encourage students to make a list of the facts they need to practice at home for homework as well as update their *Division Facts I Know* charts. In Part 1 of the Home Practice, students are reminded to bring home their *Triangle Flash Cards* for the square numbers.

Inform students when the quiz on the square numbers will be given. This quiz appears in item U.

11C Multiplying by Multiples of 10

A. $7 \times 7 =$ B. $7 \times 70 =$

C. $7 \times 700 =$ D. $7 \times 7000 =$

E. $8 \times 8 =$ F. $80 \times 8 =$

G. $800 \times 8 =$ H. $8000 \times 8 =$

Describe your method for multiplying by multiples of ten.

TIMS Bit

A. 49	B. 490
C. 4900	D. 49,000
E. 64	F. 640
G. 6400	H. 64,000

Possible response: Multiply the numbers that are not zero. Then, add on the number of zeros in both factors.

11E Missing Number

Find a number for *n* that makes the sentence true.

A. $n \times 300 = 900$ B. $7 \times n = 490$

C. $80 \times n = 640$ D. $6 \times n = 36,000$

E. $n \times 40 = 160$ F. $900 \times n = 8100$

TIMS Bit

A. 3	B. 70
C. 8	D. 6000
E. 4	F. 9

116 **Facts: The Square Numbers**

Solve and match the fact families.

A. $4 \times 4 =$
B. $7 \times 7 =$

C. $36 \div 6 =$
D. $25 \div 5 =$

E. $9 \times 9 =$
F. $64 \div 8 =$

G. $3 \times 3 =$
H. $6 \times 6 =$

I. $5 \times 5 =$
J. $9 \div 3 =$

K. $16 \div 4 =$
L. $81 \div 9 =$

M. $8 \times 8 =$
N. $49 \div 7 =$

Matches

A	K	B	___
C	___	D	___
E	___	F	___
G	___		

TIMS Bit

One strategy for solving a division fact when a student knows the dividend is a square number is just to name the divisor. $64 \div 8 = 8$. Therefore, in practicing the division facts for the square numbers it is necessary that students should continue learning through the study of the multiplication facts and fact families to ensure that they are actually gaining fluency, not just repeating the divisor.

A.	16	B.	49
C.	6	D.	5
E.	81	F.	8
G.	9	H.	36
I.	25	J.	3
K.	4	L.	9
M.	64	N.	7

A	K	B	N
C	H	D	I
E	L	F	M
G	J		

11I Fact Families for × and ÷

TIMS Bit

The following two facts belong to the same fact family.

6 × 6 = 36   36 ÷ 6 = 6

Complete this item orally as a class. One student can solve the given fact and other students can name the related fact.

Solve each fact. Then, name the other fact that is in the same fact family.

  A. 8 × 8 =

  B. 5 × 5 =

  C. 7 × 7 =

  D. 2 × 2 =

  E. 9 × 9 =

  F. 1 × 1 =

  G. 4 × 4 =

  H. 10 × 10 =

  A. 64; 64 ÷ 8 = 8

  B. 25; 25 ÷ 5 = 5

  C. 49; 49 ÷ 7 = 7

  D. 4; 4 ÷ 2 = 2

  E. 81; 81 ÷ 9 = 9

  F. 1; 1 ÷ 1 = 1

  G. 16; 16 ÷ 4 = 4

  H. 100; 100 ÷ 10 = 10

11Q More Multiplying with Multiples of 10

TIMS Bit

  A. 800 × 8 =   B. 40 × 40 =

  C. 7000 × 7 =   D. 90 × 900 =

  E. 4000 × 40 =   F. 600 × 60 =

  G. 10 × 100 =   H. 2000 × 20 =

  A. 6400   B. 1600

  C. 49,000   D. 81,000

  E. 160,000   F. 36,000

  G. 1000   H. 40,000

11T Patterns in Multiplication

Complete the table below. Then, follow these directions.

×	5	9	6	8	7
7					
8					
6					
9					
5					

1. Draw a line through the square numbers.
2. Circle each number which is a multiple of 2 and also a multiple of 3.
3. What numbers are left unmarked? Why are these numbers in the table twice?

TIMS Challenge

×	5	9	6	8	7
7	35	63	42	56	49
8	40	72	48	64	56
6	30	54	36	48	42
9	45	81	54	72	63
5	25	45	30	40	35

3. 35, 63, 56, 40, 45

These numbers are in pairs because multiplication is commutative, for example: 5 × 8 = 8 × 5. Students refer to these facts as turn-around facts.

11U   Division Quiz: Square Numbers

A. $64 \div 8 =$ B. $81 \div 9 =$

C. $49 \div 7 =$ D. $25 \div 5 =$

E. $36 \div 6 =$ F. $16 \div 4 =$

G. $100 \div 10 =$ H. $9 \div 3 =$

I. $4 \div 2 =$ J. $1 \div 1 =$

TIMS Bit

We recommend 1 minute for this quiz. Allow students to change pens after the time is up and complete the remaining problems in a different color.

After students take the quiz, have them update their *Division Facts I Know* charts.

A. 8	B. 9
C. 7	D. 5
E. 6	F. 4
G. 10	H. 3
I. 2	J. 1

Unit 11: Home Practice

Part 1 *Triangle Flash Cards: Square Numbers*

Study for the quiz on the division facts for the square numbers. Take home your *Triangle Flash Cards* and your list of facts you need to study.

Here's how to use the flash cards. Ask a family member to choose one flash card at a time. Your partner should cover one of the two small numbers. This number will be the answer to a division fact. Solve a division problem with the two uncovered numbers.

Your teacher will tell you when you will have a quiz on the division facts for the square numbers. Remember to study only those facts you cannot answer correctly and quickly.

Part 3 Multiples of 10 and 100

Do the following problems in your head. Write only the answers.

A. $9 \times 30 =$ _____   **B.** $20 \times 30 =$ _____   **C.** $20 \times 20 =$ _____

D. $900 \times 300 =$ _____   **E.** $60 \times 60 =$ _____   **F.** $40 \times 400 =$ _____

G. $70 \times 700 =$ _____   **H.** $30 \times 800 =$ _____   **I.** $5 \times 30 =$ _____

5 Facts Distribution

Division:
9s · Weeks 27-29

Math Facts Groups	Weeks	Daily Practice and Problems	Home Practice	Triangle Flash Cards	Facts Quizzes and Tests
Division Practice for the 9s	27–29	Unit 12: Items 12B, 12C, 12G, 12H, 12K–12M, 12P & 12W	Unit 12 Part 1	*Triangle Flash Cards: 9s*	DPP Item 12W is a quiz on the division facts for the 9s. The *Division Facts I Know* chart is updated.

Daily Practice and Problems

Students may solve the items individually, in groups, or as a class. The items may also be assigned for homework.

Student Questions	Teacher Notes
Division Facts: 9s	**TIMS Task**
With a partner, use your *Triangle Flash Cards: 9s* to quiz each other on the division facts for the nines. Ask your partner first to cover the numbers in the squares. Use the two uncovered numbers to solve a division fact. Separate the flash cards into three piles: those facts you know and can answer quickly, those that you can figure out with a strategy, and those that you need to learn.	The *Triangle Flash Cards: 9s* are located after the Home Practice in the *Discovery Assignment Book*. Blackline masters of all the flash cards, organized by group, are in the Generic Section and in the *Grade 4 Facts Resource Guide*. Part 1 of the Home Practice reminds students to take home the list of facts they need to study as well as their flash cards.
Then, go through the cards again and have your partner cover the numbers in the circles. Use the uncovered numbers to solve a division fact. Separate the cards into three piles again.	Inform students when the quiz on the nines will be given. This quiz appears in TIMS Bit W.
Both times through, practice the facts that are in the last two piles and make a list of these facts so that you can practice them at home.	
Circle all the facts you know and can answer quickly on your *Division Facts I Know* chart.	
Repeat this process for your partner.	

Student Questions	Teacher Notes

12C Division Facts

A. $81 \div 9 =$ B. $9 \div 9 =$

C. $63 \div 9 =$ D. $27 \div 9 =$

E. $36 \div 9 =$ F. $54 \div 9 =$

G. $18 \div 9 =$ H. $72 \div 9 =$

I. $9 \div 1 =$ J. $45 \div 9 =$

TIMS Bit

A. 9   B. 1

C. 7   D. 3

E. 4   F. 6

G. 2   H. 8

I. 9   J. 5

12G More Division Facts

Find the number *n* that makes the sentence true.

A. $72 \div 8 = n$ B. $n \div 9 = 6$

C. $n \div 9 = 5$ D. $36 \div 4 = n$

E. $27 \div n = 9$ F. $n \div 9 = 9$

G. $n \div 9 = 2$ H. $63 \div n = 9$

TIMS Bit

A. 9   B. 54

C. 45   D. 9

E. 3   F. 81

G. 18   H. 7

12H Prime Factors

1. Which of the following are prime numbers?

53   54   57   67   96   103

2. For the composite numbers, use factor trees to factor them into a product of primes. You may use a calculator to help.

TIMS Task

1. 53, 67, 103

2.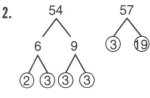

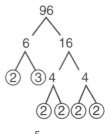

Student Questions	Teacher Notes

12K More Division Fact Practice

Find the number *n* that makes each sentence true.

A. $54 \div n = 9$

B. $720 \div n = 90$

C. $n \times 400 = 36,000$

D. $70 \times n = 63,000$

E. $90 \times n = 450$

F. $n \div 9 = 300$

TIMS Bit

A. 6

B. 8

C 90

D. 900

E. 5

F. 2700

12L Fact Practice

A. $30 \times 90 =$

B. $630 \div 70 =$

C. $360 \div 9 =$

D. $90 \times 80 =$

E. $2700 \div 9 =$

F. $9000 \times 90 =$

G. $54,000 \div 9 =$

H. $1800 \div 90 =$

I. $900 \times 0 =$

J. $900 \div 90 =$

TIMS Task

A. 2700

B. 9

C 40

D. 7200

E. 300

F. 810,000

G. 6000

H. 20

I. 0

J. 10

Student Questions	Teacher Notes

12M Fact Families for × and ÷

Solve the given fact. Then, name another fact that is in the same fact family.

  A. 9 × 8 =

  B. 54 ÷ 9 =

  C. 36 ÷ 4 =

  D. 9 × 7 =

TIMS Bit

Complete this item orally as a class. One student can solve the given fact and another student can name a related fact. The answers and possible related facts are:

  A. 72; 72 ÷ 9 = 8

  B. 6; 6 × 9 = 54

  C. 9; 4 × 9 = 36

  D. 63; 63 ÷ 7 = 9

12P Division Stories

Write a division story for 28 ÷ 9. Draw a picture for your story and write a number sentence that describes it. In your story, explain any remainder.

TIMS Task

Stories and pictures will vary. Students should label their pictures with the number sentence.

28 ÷ 9 = 3 R1 or
3 × 9 + 1 = 28

12W Division Quiz: 9s

A. 72 ÷ 9 =

B. 63 ÷ 9 =

C. 54 ÷ 9 =

D. 36 ÷ 9 =

E. 81 ÷ 9 =

F. 45 ÷ 9 =

G. 9 ÷ 9 =

H. 27 ÷ 9 =

I. 18 ÷ 9 =

TIMS Bit

A. 8	B. 7
C. 6	D. 4
E. 9	F. 5
G. 1	H. 3
I. 2	

We recommend 1 minute for this quiz. Allow students to change pens after the time is up and complete the remaining problems in a different color. After students take the test, have them update their *Division Facts I Know* charts.

Since students learned the division facts through work with fact families, it is likely that the student who answers 72 ÷ 9 correctly also knows the answer to 72 ÷ 8. To make sure, however, after the quiz, ask students to write a related division fact for each of the facts on the quiz. A student who answers a given fact correctly and who also writes the correct related fact can circle both facts on the chart.

Unit 12: Home Practice

Part 1 Triangle Flash Cards: 9s

Study for the quiz on the division facts for the nines. Take home your *Triangle Flash Cards: 9s* and your list of facts you need to study.

Ask a family member to choose one flash card at a time. He or she should cover one of the smaller numbers. (One of the smaller numbers is circled. The other has a square around it.) Solve a division fact using the two uncovered numbers. Ask your family member to sometimes cover the circled numbers and sometimes cover the number in the square.

Your teacher will tell you when the quiz on the nines will be.

Facts Distribution
Division:
The Last Six Facts · Weeks 30-32

Math Facts Groups	Weeks	Daily Practice and Problems	Home Practice	Triangle Flash Cards	Facts Quizzes and Tests
Division Practice for The Last Six Facts	30–32	Unit 13: Items 13B–13D, 13H, 13K, 13Q, 13S & 13U	Unit 13 Part 1	*Triangle Flash Cards: The Last Six Facts*	DPP Item 13S is a quiz on the division facts for The Last Six Facts. The *Division Facts I Know* chart is updated.

Students may solve the items individually, in groups, or as a class. The items may also be assigned for homework.

Student Questions	Teacher Notes

 The Last Six Facts

With a partner, use your *Triangle Flash Cards: Last Six Facts* to quiz each other on the related division facts for the last six multiplication facts (24 ÷ 6, 24 ÷ 4, 28 ÷ 7, 28 ÷ 4, 32 ÷ 8, 32 ÷ 4, 42 ÷ 7, 42 ÷ 6, 48 ÷ 8, 48 ÷ 6, 56 ÷ 8, 56 ÷ 7). Ask your partner first to cover the numbers in the squares. Use the two uncovered numbers to solve a division fact. Then, ask your partner to cover the numbers in the circles. Use the uncovered numbers to solve a division fact.

After each time through the cards, separate them into three piles: those facts you know and can answer quickly, those that you can figure out with a strategy, and those that you need to learn. Practice the last two piles again and then make a list of the facts you need to practice at home for homework.

Circle the facts you know and can answer quickly on your *Division Facts I Know* chart.

TIMS Task

The flash cards for the last six facts can be found after the Home Practice in the *Discovery Assignment Book* and in the *Unit Resource Guide* Generic Section. Discuss strategies students use to find the answers to the facts, emphasizing those strategies that are more efficient than others.

In Part 1 of the Home Practice, students are reminded to bring home their *Triangle Flash Cards: Last Six Facts*.

Inform students when the quiz on the last six facts will be. This quiz appears in item S.

Student Questions	Teacher Notes

13C Multiplication Facts Review

A. $8 \times 4 =$ B. $7 \times 4 =$

C. $6 \times 7 =$ D. $7 \times 8 =$

E. $6 \times 8 =$ F. $4 \times 6 =$

TIMS Bit

Discuss strategies students use to solve the facts, emphasizing those strategies that are more efficient than others. Students might use a fact they know to solve another. For example, to solve 6×7, students might first think 5×7 is 35. Then, adding on one more 7 to 35 will give 42. Students who know the square numbers well might use the square numbers to solve "close" facts. For example, to solve 7×8, first think "7×7 is 49." Then, add 7 to 49 to get 56. Students may also say, "I just know it." Recall is obviously an efficient strategy.

13D Fact Families for $\times$ and $\div$

The following four facts belong to the same fact family.

$4 \times 6 = 24$ $6 \times 4 = 24$

$24 \div 6 = 4$ $24 \div 4 = 6$

Solve each fact. Then, name three other facts that are in the same fact family.

A. $28 \div 7 =$

B. $7 \times 8 =$

C. $7 \times 6 =$

D. $32 \div 4 =$

E. $8 \times 6 =$

TIMS Task

Complete this item orally as a class. One student can solve the given fact and other students can name each of the other related facts.

A. 4; $28 \div 4 = 7$
   $7 \times 4 = 28$
   $4 \times 7 = 28$

B. 56; $8 \times 7 = 56$
   $56 \div 8 = 7$
   $56 \div 7 = 8$

C. 42; $6 \times 7 = 42$
   $42 \div 7 = 6$
   $42 \div 6 = 7$

D. 8; $32 \div 8 = 4$
   $8 \times 4 = 32$
   $4 \times 8 = 32$

E. 48; $6 \times 8 = 48$
   $48 \div 6 = 8$
   $48 \div 8 = 6$

13H Multiples of 10 and 100

Solve each pair of related number sentences.

A. $4 \times 80 =$ and $320 \div 4 =$

B. $40 \times 6 =$ and $240 \div 40 =$

C. $70 \times 4 =$ and $280 \div 70 =$

D. $60 \times 7 =$ and $420 \div 7 =$

E. $8 \times 70 =$ and $560 \div 70 =$

F. $80 \times 60 =$ and $4800 \div 80 =$

TIMS Task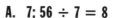

A. 320; 80
B. 240; 6
C. 280; 4
D. 420; 60
E. 560; 8
F. 4800; 60

13K Related Division Facts

Solve each fact. Then, name the other division fact in the same fact family.

A. $56 \div 8 =$

B. $32 \div 4 =$

C. $42 \div 7 =$

D. $24 \div 4 =$

E. $48 \div 6 =$

F. $28 \div 7 =$

TIMS Bit

A. $7; 56 \div 7 = 8$
B. $8; 32 \div 8 = 4$
C. $6; 42 \div 6 = 7$
D. $6; 24 \div 6 = 4$
E. $8; 48 \div 8 = 6$
F. $4; 28 \div 4 = 7$

Student Questions	Teacher Notes

13Q Division Practice

A. $60 \div 8 =$

B. $25 \div 4 =$

C. $35 \div 8 =$

D. $50 \div 6 =$

E. $30 \div 7 =$

F. $45 \div 6 =$

A. 7 R4

B. 6 R1

C. 4 R3

D. 8 R2

E. 4 R2

F. 7 R3

13S Facts Quiz: Last Six Facts

TIMS Bit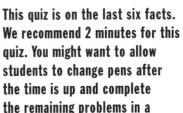

A. $24 \div 6 =$ B. $28 \div 7 =$

C. $56 \div 7 =$ D. $32 \div 8 =$

E. $48 \div 8 =$ F. $24 \div 4 =$

G. $42 \div 6 =$ H. $32 \div 4 =$

I. $48 \div 6 =$ J. $56 \div 8 =$

K. $28 \div 4 =$ L. $42 \div 7 =$

This quiz is on the last six facts. We recommend 2 minutes for this quiz. You might want to allow students to change pens after the time is up and complete the remaining problems in a different color.

After students take the test, have them update their *Division Facts I Know* charts.

13U Zero and Division

TIMS Bit

Solve the following. Justify your reasoning using a related multiplication sentence.

A. $7 \div 0 =$ B. $0 \div 0 =$

C. $0 \div 7 =$ D. $7 \div 1 =$

A. $7 \div 0$ is undefined since there is no number that makes $0 \times ? = 7$ a true statement.

B. $0 \div 0$ is undefined since there is no one number that makes $0 \times ? = 0$ true.

C. $0 \div 7 = 0$ since $0 \times 7 = 0$.

D. $7 \div 1 = 7$ since $1 \times 7 = 7$.

Unit 13: Home Practice

Part 1 Triangle Flash Cards: Last Six Facts

Study for the quiz on the division facts for the last six facts ($24 \div 6$, $24 \div 4$, $28 \div 7$, $28 \div 4$, $32 \div 8$, $32 \div 4$, $42 \div 7$, $42 \div 6$, $48 \div 8$, $48 \div 6$, $56 \div 8$, $56 \div 7$). Take home your *Triangle Flash Cards* and your list of facts you need to study.

Here's how to use the flash cards. Ask a family member to choose one flash card at a time. Your partner should cover the corner containing either the square or the circle. This number will be the answer to a division fact. Solve a division fact with the two uncovered numbers.

Your teacher will tell you when the quiz on these facts will be. Remember to study only those facts you cannot answer correctly and quickly.

5 Facts Distribution
Division: 2s, 5s, 10s, and Square Numbers · Week 33

Math Facts Groups	Week	Daily Practice and Problems	Home Practice	Triangle Flash Cards	Facts Quizzes and Tests
Division Review for the 2s, 5s, 10s, and the Square Numbers	33	Unit 14: Items 14A–14C, 14G, 14K, 14M & 14*O*	Unit 14 Part 1	*Triangle Flash Cards: 2s, 5s, 10s,* and the *Square Numbers*	DPP Item 14M and 14*O* are quizzes on the division facts for the 2s, 5s, 10s, and the Square Numbers. The *Division Facts I Know* chart is updated.

Students may solve the items individually, in groups, or as a class. The items may also be assigned for homework.

Student Questions	Teacher Notes
14A **Guess My Number**	**TIMS Bit** ⬛⬛ 1. 54 2. "I am not prime." Since the number is a multiple of 2 and 3, the number cannot be prime. 3. 6

14A **Guess My Number**

I am a multiple of 2 and 3.

I am less than 63 but greater than 48.

I am not prime.

I am not a multiple of 10.

1. What number am I?

2. What clue above is redundant or unnecessary?

3. If I'm a multiple of 2 and 3, I must be a multiple of what other number?

14B Division Facts

TIMS Task

With a partner, use your *Triangle Flash Cards* to quiz each other on the division facts for the 5s, 10s, 2s, and square numbers. One partner covers the corner with the number in a circle. This number will be the answer to a division fact, called the quotient. The second person uses the two uncovered numbers to solve a division fact.

Go through the cards again. This time the first person covers the number in the square and the second solves a division fact using the two uncovered numbers.

Each time through the cards, separate them into three piles: those facts you know and can answer quickly, those that you can figure out with a strategy, and those that you need to learn. Practice the last two piles again and then make a list of the facts you need to practice at home for homework.

Circle the facts you know and can answer quickly on your *Division Facts I Know* chart.

The flash cards for these groups of facts can be found in the *Unit Resource Guide* Generic Section and the *Grade 4 Facts Resource Guide*. They were distributed in Units 8, 10, and 11 in the *Discovery Assignment Book*. Students will need the flash cards to review all the facts again in Unit 16.

Students make a list of the facts they need to practice at home for homework as well as update their *Division Facts I Know* charts. In Part 1 of the Home Practice, students are reminded to bring home their *Triangle Flash Cards* to study.

Inform students when the two quizzes on the facts will be. These quizzes appear in items M and 0.

14C More Division Facts

A. $90 \div 9 =$	B. $6 \div 3 =$
C. $9 \div 3 =$	D. $40 \div 10 =$
E. $20 \div 2 =$	F. $64 \div 8 =$
G. $8 \div 4 =$	H. $10 \div 2 =$
I. $36 \div 6 =$	J. $70 \div 7 =$
K. $10 \div 5 =$	L. $18 \div 9 =$
M. $16 \div 8 =$	N. $5 \div 5 =$
O. $50 \div 5 =$	P. $25 \div 5 =$
Q. $15 \div 3 =$	R. $4 \div 2 =$

TIMS Bit

A.	10	B.	2
C.	3	D.	4
E.	10	F.	8
G.	2	H.	5
I.	6	J.	10
K.	2	L.	2
M.	2	N.	1
O.	10	P.	5
Q.	5	R.	2

146 Fact Families for × and ÷

The following four facts belong to the same fact family.

$4 \times 2 = 8$ $2 \times 4 = 8$
$8 \div 2 = 4$ $8 \div 4 = 2$

Solve each fact. Then, name the other facts that are in the same fact family.

A. $12 \div 2 =$ B. $6 \times 5 =$

C. $9 \times 9 =$ D. $60 \div 6 =$

E. $2 \times 7 =$ F. $20 \div 5 =$

G. $9 \times 5 =$ H. $8 \times 10 =$

I. $16 \div 4 =$ J. $49 \div 7 =$

K. $40 \div 8 =$ L. $8 \times 8 =$

M. $10 \times 10 =$ N. $5 \times 7 =$

TIMS Bit

Complete this item orally as a class. One student can solve the given fact and other students can name each of the other related facts.

A. $6; 12 \div 6 = 2$
    $6 \times 2 = 12$
    $2 \times 6 = 12$

B. $30; 5 \times 6 = 30$
    $30 \div 6 = 5$
    $30 \div 5 = 6$

C. 81
    $81 \div 9 = 9$

D. $10; 60 \div 10 = 6$
    $6 \times 10 = 60$
    $10 \times 6 = 60$

E. $14; 7 \times 2 = 14$
    $14 \div 7 = 2$
    $14 \div 2 = 7$

F. $4; 20 \div 4 = 5$
    $4 \times 5 = 20$
    $5 \times 4 = 20$

G. $45; 5 \times 9 = 45$
    $45 \div 5 = 9$
    $45 \div 9 = 5$

H. $80; 10 \times 8 = 80$
    $80 \div 8 = 10$
    $80 \div 10 = 8$

I. $4; 4 \times 4 = 16$

J. $7; 7 \times 7 = 49$

K. $5; 40 \div 5 = 8$
    $5 \times 8 = 40$
    $8 \times 5 = 40$

L. $64; 64 \div 8 = 8$

M. $100; 100 \div 10 = 10$

N. $35; 7 \times 5 = 35$
    $35 \div 7 = 5$
    $35 \div 5 = 7$

Still More Division Facts

Complete the table using division. Use the number in the first column as your divisor. Write your answer (the quotient) in the empty boxes.

÷	10	20	30	40	50	100
2						
5						
10						

What patterns do you see?

TIMS Bit

÷	10	20	30	40	50	100
2	5	10	15	20	25	50
5	2	4	6	8	10	20
10	1	2	3	4	5	10

14M Division Facts Quiz 1

A. 35 ÷ 7 =   B. 64 ÷ 8 =

C. 14 ÷ 2 =   D. 80 ÷ 8 =

E. 8 ÷ 4 =   F. 16 ÷ 4 =

G. 50 ÷ 10 =   H. 36 ÷ 6 =

I. 9 ÷ 3 =   J. 100 ÷ 10 =

K. 30 ÷ 5 =   L. 40 ÷ 4 =

M. 18 ÷ 9 =   N. 6 ÷ 2 =

O. 25 ÷ 5 =   P. 5 ÷ 5 =

TIMS Bit

This quiz is the first of two quizzes on the division facts for the 5s, 10s, 2s, and square numbers. Half of the facts are in this quiz and half appear in the second quiz in item O. We recommend 2 minutes for this quiz. Allow students to change pens after the time is up and complete the remaining problems in a different color.

After students take the quiz, have them update their *Division Facts I Know* charts.

Since students learned the division facts through work with fact families, it is likely that the student who answers 35 ÷ 7 correctly also knows the answer to 35 ÷ 5. To make sure, however, ask students to write a related division fact for each of the facts on the quiz (except the square numbers). A student who answers a given fact correctly and who also writes the correct related fact can circle both facts on the chart.

140 Division Facts Quiz 2

A. $10 \div 1 =$ B. $40 \div 8 =$

C. $10 \div 5 =$ D. $49 \div 7 =$

E. $70 \div 7 =$ F. $16 \div 8 =$

G. $4 \div 2 =$ H. $15 \div 5 =$

I. $20 \div 5 =$ J. $81 \div 9 =$

K. $45 \div 9 =$ L. $30 \div 3 =$

M. $12 \div 6 =$ N. $60 \div 10 =$

O. $20 \div 2 =$ P. $90 \div 9 =$

TIMS Bit

This quiz is on the division facts for the 5s, 10s, 2s, and square numbers. Half of the facts are on this quiz. Half appear on the quiz in item M. We recommend 2 minutes for this quiz. Allow students to change pens after the time is up and complete the remaining problems in a different color.

After students take the quiz, have them update their *Division Facts I Know* charts.

It is likely that the student who answers $40 \div 8$ correctly also knows $40 \div 5$. To make sure, ask students to write the related division fact for each fact on the quiz (except the square numbers). A student who answers a given fact correctly and who also writes the given related division fact correctly can circle both facts on the chart.

Unit 14: Home Practice

Part 1 *Triangle Flash Cards: 2s, 5s, 10s, and Square Numbers*

Study for the quizzes on the division facts. Take home your *Triangle Flash Cards* and your list of facts you need to study.

Here's how to use the flash cards. Ask a family member to choose one flash card at a time. Your partner should cover the corner with the circle. This number will be the answer to a division fact, called the quotient. Use the two uncovered numbers to solve a division fact. Then have your partner go through the cards covering the corner with a square. Use the two uncovered numbers to solve a division fact.

Your teacher will tell you when the quiz on the facts will be. Remember to study only those facts you cannot answer correctly and quickly.

Facts Distribution
Division: 3s, 9s, and The Last Six Facts · Week 34

Math Facts Groups	Week	Daily Practice and Problems	Home Practice	Triangle Flash Cards	Facts Quizzes and Tests
Division Review for the 3s, 9s, and The Last Six Facts	34	Unit 15: Items 15B, 15E, 15G, 15J, 15L, 15M & 15O	Unit 15 Parts 1 & 2	*Triangle Flash Cards: 3s, 9s,* and *The Last Six Facts*	DPP Items 15M and 15O are quizzes on the division facts for the 3s, 9s, and The Last Six Facts. The *Division Facts I Know* chart is updated.

Students may solve the items individually, in groups, or as a class. The items may also be assigned for homework.

Student Questions	Teacher Notes

 Division Facts

With a partner, use your *Triangle Flash Cards* to quiz each other on the division facts for the threes, nines, and the 12 related division facts for the last six multiplication facts (4×6, 4×7, 4×8, 6×7, 6×8, 7×8). One partner covers the corner with a square with his or her thumb. This number will be the answer to a division fact, called the quotient. The second person divides the two uncovered numbers. Repeat the process, this time covering the corner with a circle.

Each time through the cards, separate them into three piles: those facts you know and can answer quickly, those that you can figure out with a strategy, and those that you need to learn. Practice the last two piles again and then make a list of the facts you need to practice at home for homework.

Circle the facts you know and can answer quickly on your *Division Facts I Know* chart.

TIMS Task

For those students who need new copies of the *Triangle Flash Cards*, masters for the flash cards can be found in the *Unit Resource Guide* Generic Section. After students sort the cards, they should be encouraged to practice the facts in the last two piles—those facts that they can figure out with a strategy and those they need to learn. Discuss strategies students use to find the answers to the facts, emphasizing those strategies that are more efficient than others.

Students make a list of the facts they need to practice at home for homework as well as update their *Division Facts I Know* charts. In Part 1 of the Home Practice, students are reminded to bring home their *Triangle Flash Cards*.

Inform students when the two quizzes on the facts will be. Half of the facts appear in item M. The others appear in item O.

15E Multiplying and Dividing by Multiples of 10

A. $500 \times 30 =$ B. $60 \times 4 =$

C. $50 \times 90 =$ D. $0 \times 300 =$

E. $2400 \div 8 =$ F. $900 \div 9 =$

G. $30 \div 10 =$ H. $1800 \div 2 =$

I. $210 \div 30 =$ J. $1200 \div 40 =$

K. $60 \times 700 =$ L. $0 \div 9 =$

A. 15,000   B. 240

C. 4500   D. 0

E. 300   F. 100

G. 3   H. 900

I. 7   J. 30

K. 42,000   L. 0

15G Fact Families for × and ÷

Solve each fact. Then, name the three other facts that are in the same fact family. (The square numbers only have two facts in each family.)

A. $6 \times 8 =$ B. $18 \div 6 =$

C. $81 \div 9 =$ D. $9 \times 8 =$

E. $4 \times 7 =$ F. $3 \times 2 =$

G. $32 \div 4 =$ H. $7 \times 6 =$

I. $9 \div 3 =$ J. $27 \div 3 =$

K. $9 \times 1 =$

TIMS Bit

Complete this item orally as a class. One student can solve the given fact and other students can name each of the other related facts.

A. 48; $8 \times 6 = 48$
   $48 \div 6 = 8$
   $48 \div 8 = 6$

B. 3; $18 \div 3 = 6$
   $6 \times 3 = 18$
   $3 \times 6 = 18$

C. 9; $9 \times 9 = 81$

D. 72; $8 \times 9 = 72$
   $72 \div 8 = 9$
   $72 \div 9 = 8$

E. 28; $7 \times 4 = 28$
   $28 \div 4 = 7$
   $28 \div 7 = 4$

F. 6; $2 \times 3 = 6$
   $6 \div 3 = 2$
   $6 \div 2 = 3$

G. 8; $32 \div 8 = 4$
   $4 \times 8 = 32$
   $8 \times 4 = 32$

H. 42; $42 \div 7 = 6$
   $42 \div 6 = 7$
   $6 \times 7 = 42$

I. 3; $3 \times 3 = 9$

J. 9; $27 \div 9 = 3$
   $3 \times 9 = 27$
   $9 \times 3 = 27$

K. 9; $1 \times 9 = 9$
   $9 \div 1 = 9$
   $9 \div 9 = 1$

15J Function Machine: Order of Operations

Complete the following table. Make sure you follow the correct order of operations.

Input	Output
1	
2	
3	
4	
5	
6	
7	
N	$10 + 3 \times N$

TIMS Task

You may need to remind students to multiply the input number by 3 before adding 10.

Input	Output
1	13
2	16
3	19
4	22
5	25
6	28
7	31
N	$10 + 3 \times N$

15L Related Multiplication and Division Sentences

Find a number for n in each number sentence that makes the statement true.

1. $4 \times n = 2400$ $2400 \div 4 = n$

2. $n \times 9 = 360$ $360 \div 9 = n$

3. $7 \times n = 63{,}000$ $63{,}000 \div 7 = n$

4. $6 \times n = 54$ $54 \div 6 = n$

5. $9 \times n = 4500$ $4500 \div 9 = n$

6. $8 \times n = 560$ $560 \div 8 = n$

7. $3 \times n = 0$ $0 \div 3 = n$

TIMS Task

1. $n = 600$

2. $n = 40$

3. $n = 9000$

4. $n = 9$

5. $n = 500$

6. $n = 70$

7. $n = 0$

Student Questions	Teacher Notes

15M Division Facts Quiz 1

A. $90 \div 9 =$ B. $6 \div 3 =$

C. $3 \div 3 =$ D. $48 \div 8 =$

E. $15 \div 5 =$ F. $63 \div 7 =$

G. $32 \div 4 =$ H. $18 \div 9 =$

I. $9 \div 3 =$ J. $9 \div 1 =$

K. $36 \div 4 =$ L. $42 \div 7 =$

M. $54 \div 9 =$ N. $24 \div 3 =$

TIMS Bit

This quiz is on the division facts for the threes, nines, and last six facts. Half of the facts are on this quiz. Half appear in the quiz in Bit O. We recommend 2 minutes for this quiz. Allow students to change pens after the time is up and complete the remaining problems in a different color.

After students take the quiz, have them update their *Division Facts I Know* charts. It is likely that the student who knows $90 \div 9$ also knows $90 \div 10$. To make sure, ask students to write the related division fact for each fact on the quiz (except the square numbers). A student who answers a given fact correctly and who also writes the related division fact correctly can circle both facts on the chart.

15O Division Facts Quiz 2

A. $27 \div 9 =$ B. $28 \div 7 =$

C. $12 \div 3 =$ D. $24 \div 6 =$

E. $56 \div 8 =$ F. $81 \div 9 =$

G. $21 \div 3 =$ H. $30 \div 10 =$

I. $45 \div 9 =$ J. $72 \div 9 =$

K. $24 \div 3 =$ L. $3 \div 3 =$

M. $0 \div 9 =$ N. $18 \div 3 =$

TIMS Bit

This quiz is on the division facts for the threes, nines, and last six facts. Half of the facts are on this quiz. Half were in the quiz in Bit M. We recommend 2 minutes for this quiz. Allow students to change pens after the time is up and complete the remaining problems in a different color.

After students take the quiz, have them update their *Division Facts I Know* charts. It is likely that the student who knows $27 \div 9$ also knows $27 \div 3$. To make sure, ask students to write the related division fact for each fact on the quiz (except the square numbers). A student who answers a given fact correctly and who also writes the related division fact correctly can circle both facts on the chart.

Unit 15: Home Practice

Part 1 Triangle Flash Cards: 3s, 9s, Last Six Facts

Study for the two quizzes on the division facts. Half the facts will be on the first quiz. The other half will be on the second quiz. Take home your *Triangle Flash Cards* and your list of facts you need to study.

Here's how to use the flash cards. Ask a family member to choose one flash card at a time. Your partner should cover the corner with a square. This number will be the answer to a division fact. Divide the two uncovered numbers. Go through cards again, but this time cover the number in the circle.

Your teacher will tell you when the quizzes on the facts will be. Remember to study only those facts you cannot answer correctly and quickly.

Part 2 Mixed-Up Multiplication Tables

I. Complete the tables.

A.

×	3	4	6	7	8
4					
6		24			
7					
8					

B.

×	0	1	5	7	9
3					
6			30		
9					
10					

2. Solve each fact. Then, on a separate sheet of paper, name three other facts that are in the same fact family. For example, the following four facts are in the same fact family: $3 \times 6 = 18$, $6 \times 3 = 18$, $18 \div 3 = 6$, and $18 \div 6 = 3$. (Remember, the square numbers only have two facts in each family.)

A. $8 \times 4 =$ _____   **B.** $81 \div 9 =$ _____   **C.** $7 \times 6 =$ _____

D. $9 \times 4 =$ _____   **E.** $21 \div 7 =$ _____   **F.** $10 \times 9 =$ _____

G. $3 \times 3 =$ _____   **H.** $56 \div 7 =$ _____   **I.** $6 \times 9 =$ _____

Facts Distribution
Division:
All Fact Groups · Weeks 35-36

Math Facts Groups	Weeks	Daily Practice and Problems	Home Practice	Triangle Flash Cards	Facts Quizzes and Tests
Division Review and Assessment for All Fact Groups	35–36	Unit 16: Items 16B, 16C, 16I, 16O, 16P & 16R	Unit 16 Parts 1 & 2	*Triangle Flash Cards: 5s, 10s, 2s, 3s, Square Numbers, 9s,* and *The Last Six Facts*	DPP Item 16R is an inventory test on all five groups of division facts. The *Division Facts I Know* chart is updated.

Students may solve the items individually, in groups, or as a class. The items may also be assigned for homework.

Student Questions	Teacher Notes

 Division Facts

With a partner, use your *Triangle Flash Cards* to quiz each other on all the division facts. One partner covers the corner containing the number in a square with his or her thumb. The second person solves a division fact using the two uncovered numbers. Go through the cards a second time, this time covering the corner containing the number in a circle.

After each time through the cards, separate them into three piles: those facts you know and can answer quickly, those that you can figure out with a strategy, and those that you need to study. Practice the last two piles again and then make a list of the facts you need to practice at home for homework.

Circle the facts you know and can answer quickly on your *Division Facts I Know* chart.

TIMS Task

Students used the flash cards to review all five groups of facts in Units 14 and 15. For those students who need new copies, masters for the flash cards can be found in the *Unit Resource Guide* Generic Section. After students sort the cards, they should continue to practice the facts in the last two piles—those facts that they can figure out with a strategy and those they need to learn. Discuss strategies students use to find the answers to the facts, emphasizing those strategies that are more efficient than others.

Encourage students to make a list of the facts they need to practice at home for homework as well as update their *Division Facts I Know* chart. In Part 1 of the Home Practice, students are reminded to bring home their *Triangle Flash Cards* for the division facts.

An inventory test on all the facts is given in DPP item R. Inform students when the test will be given.

16C Division Facts Practice

1. A. $50 \div 5 =$ B. $12 \div 3 =$

     C. $90 \div 10 =$ D. $0 \div 8 =$

     E. $24 \div 8 =$ F. $28 \div 7 =$

     G. $56 \div 8 =$ H. $80 \div 8 =$

     I. $4 \div 4 =$ J. $48 \div 8 =$

2. Explain your strategy for Question 1G.

TIMS Bit

1. A. 10
   B. 4
   C. 9
   D. 0
   E. 3
   F. 4
   G. 7
   H. 10
   I. 1
   J. 6

2. Strategies will vary.

16I Fact Families for × and ÷

Solve each fact. Then, name the three other facts that are in the same fact family. The square numbers have only two facts in each family.

A. $8 \times 3 =$

B. $30 \div 6 =$

C. $64 \div 8 =$

D. $9 \times 7 =$

E. $24 \div 4 =$

F. $6 \times 6 =$

G. $36 \div 4 =$

H. $8 \times 4 =$

I. $42 \div 7 =$

J. $6 \times 9 =$

TIMS Bit

Complete this item orally as a class. One student can solve the given fact and other students can name each of the other related facts.

A. $24; 3 \times 8 = 24;$
   $24 \div 3 = 8; 24 \div 8 = 3$

B. $5; 30 \div 5 = 6;$
   $5 \times 6 = 30; 6 \times 5 = 30$

C. $8; 8 \times 8 = 64$

D. $63; 7 \times 9 = 63;$
   $63 \div 7 = 9; 63 \div 9 = 7$

E. $6; 24 \div 6 = 4;$
   $6 \times 4 = 24; 4 \times 6 = 24$

F. $36; 36 \div 6 = 6$

G. $9; 36 \div 9 = 4;$
   $4 \times 9 = 36; 9 \times 4 = 36$

H. $32; 4 \times 8 = 32;$
   $32 \div 4 = 8; 32 \div 8 = 4$

I. $6; 42 \div 6 = 7;$
   $6 \times 7 = 42; 7 \times 6 = 42$

J. $54; 9 \times 6 = 54;$
   $54 \div 9 = 6; 54 \div 6 = 9$

Student Questions	Teacher Notes

16O Multiplying with Zeros

The *n* in each number sentence stands for a missing number. Find the number that makes each sentence true.

A. $80 \times n = 320$

B. $n \times 30 = 27{,}000$

C. $8000 \times n = 56{,}000$

D. $50 \times n = 10{,}000$

E. $400 \times n = 40{,}000$

F. $300 \times n = 1500$

TIMS Bit

A. 4

B. 900

C. 7

D. 200

E. 100

F. 5

16P Zeros and Ones

1. A. $8 \times 1 =$ B. $4 \div 0 =$

    C. $0 \div 9 =$ D. $1 \div 1 =$

    E. $12 \div 1 =$ F. $5 \div 0 =$

    G. $7 \times 0 =$ H. $3 \div 3 =$

2. Justify your reasoning for Questions 1B and 1C using a related multiplication sentence.

TIMS Task

1. A. 8   B. Undefined

    C. 0   D. 1

    E. 12   F. undefined

    G. 0   H. 1

2. B. There is no number that makes $? \times 0 = 4$ true.

    C. $9 \times 0 = 0$

16R Division Facts Inventory Test

Have two pens or pencils of different colors ready. During the first four minutes of the test, write the answers using one color pen or pencil. After four minutes have passed, complete the remaining items with the other color pen or pencil.

TIMS Task

Students take the *Division Facts Inventory Test.* We recommend four minutes for this test. Allow students to change to different colored pencils or pens after four minutes and complete the test.

Since students learned the division facts through their work with fact families, if a student knows $27 \div 3 = 9$, he or she most likely knows that $27 \div 9 = 3$. To make sure, after the test ask students to write a related division fact for each fact on the test (other than the facts for the square numbers). Students then update their *Division Facts I Know* charts for the last time and place both this test and the chart in their portfolios.

1. 2	2. 8	3. 2	4. 8
5. 8	6. 5	7. 4	8. 3
9. 3	10. 3	11. 3	12. 10
13. 3	14. 7	15. 9	16. 6
17. 8	18. 7	19. 9	20. 5
21. 10	22. 4	23. 9	24. 2
25. 2	26. 8	27. 2	28. 10
29. 5	30. 0	31. 8	32. 6
33. 4	34. 9	35. 6	36. 5
37. 8	38. 10	39. 7	40. 3
41. 5	42. 6	43. 1	44. 3
45. 5	46. 5	47. 10	48. 6

Division Facts Inventory Test

1. $18 \div 9 =$ 2. $40 \div 5 =$ 3. $4 \div 2 =$ 4. $80 \div 10 =$

5. $72 \div 9 =$ 6. $30 \div 6 =$ 7. $12 \div 3 =$ 8. $21 \div 7 =$

9. $6 \div 2 =$ 10. $18 \div 6 =$ 11. $27 \div 9 =$ 12. $40 \div 4 =$

13. $9 \div 3 =$ 14. $35 \div 5 =$ 15. $63 \div 7 =$ 16. $48 \div 8 =$

17. $32 \div 4 =$ 18. $42 \div 6 =$ 19. $36 \div 4 =$ 20. $5 \div 1 =$

21. $90 \div 9 =$ 22. $16 \div 4 =$ 23. $81 \div 9 =$ 24. $16 \div 8 =$

25. $8 \div 4 =$ 26. $24 \div 3 =$ 27. $14 \div 7 =$ 28. $100 \div 10 =$

29. $10 \div 2 =$ 30. $0 \div 9 =$ 31. $64 \div 8 =$ 32. $60 \div 10 =$

33. $28 \div 7 =$ 34. $54 \div 6 =$ 35. $36 \div 6 =$ 36. $45 \div 9 =$

37. $56 \div 7 =$ 38. $20 \div 2 =$ 39. $49 \div 7 =$ 40. $30 \div 10 =$

41. $25 \div 5 =$ 42. $24 \div 4 =$ 43. $7 \div 7 =$ 44. $15 \div 5 =$

45. $20 \div 4 =$ 46. $50 \div 10 =$ 47. $70 \div 7 =$ 48. $12 \div 2 =$

Name _____ Date _____

Unit 16: Home Practice

Part 1 Triangle Flash Cards: All the Facts

Study for the test on all the division facts. Take home your *Triangle Flash Cards* and your list of facts you need to study.

Here's how to use the flash cards. Ask a family member to choose one flash card at a time. Your partner should cover the corner containing the number in a square. This number will be the answer to a division fact. Solve a division fact with the two uncovered numbers. Go through the cards a second time, this time covering the numbers in the circle.

Your teacher will tell you when the test on all the facts will be. Remember to concentrate on those facts you cannot answer correctly and quickly.

Part 2 Multiplication Tables

Complete the following tables.

1.

×	7	4	6	2	9
8					
3		12			
5					
1					

2.

×	10	5	6	3	0
8					
4		20			
2					
1					

3. Complete the following. Remember to follow the correct order of operations. Do all multiplications before any addition and subtraction. For example,
   $4 + 100 \times 3 =$
   $4 + 300 = 304.$

   A. $7 \times 100 + 3 =$ _____

   B. $6 + 800 \times 7 =$ _____

   C. $5000 - 400 \times 5 =$ _____

   D. $20 \times 20 + 350 =$ _____

   E. $600 \times 80 - 2000 =$ _____

   F. $20{,}000 - 18{,}000 \times 1 =$ _____

Section
6
Math Facts Games

This section contains games and activities that provide practice with the multiplication and division facts.

Floor Tiler

This game can be played by two or more players.

Materials

- $\frac{1}{2}$ sheet of *Centimeter Grid Paper*
- *Spinners 1–4 and 1–10* Activity Page
- A clear plastic spinner or a paper clip and pencil
- A crayon or marker for each player

Rules

1. The first player makes two spins so that he or she has two numbers. The player may either spin one spinner twice or spin each spinner once.

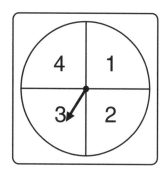
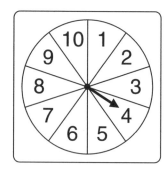

2. The player must then find the **product** of the two numbers he or she spun. For example, $3 \times 4 = $ **12.** 12 is the product. The product is the answer to a multiplication problem.

3. After finding the product, the player colors in a rectangle that has the same number of grid squares on the grid paper. For example, he or she might color in 3 rows of 4 squares for a total of 12 squares. But the player could also color in 2 rows of 6 squares or 1 row of 12 squares. (Remember, the squares colored in must connect so that they form a rectangle.)

4. Once the player has made his or her rectangle, the player draws an outline around it and writes its number sentence inside. For example, a player who colored in 3 rows of 4 squares would write "$3 \times 4 = 12$." A player who colored in 2 rows of 6 squares would write "$2 \times 6 = 12$."

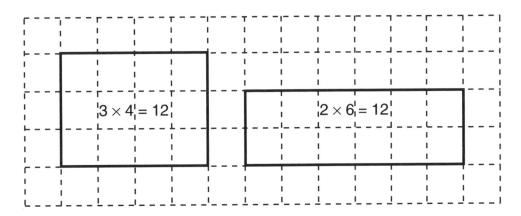

5. Players take turns spinning and filling in their grids.

6. If a player is unable to fill in a rectangle for his or her spin, that player loses the turn, and the next player can play.

7. The first player to fill in his or her grid paper completely wins the game.

Name _____   Date _____

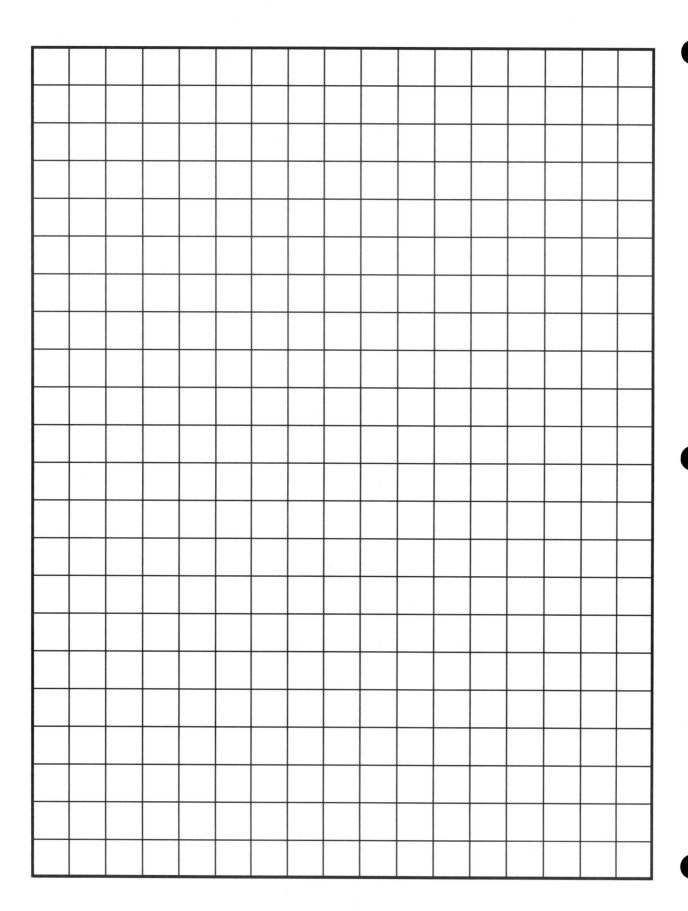

Grade 4 · Facts Resource Guide · Section 6 · Math Facts Games

Spinners 1-4 and 1-10

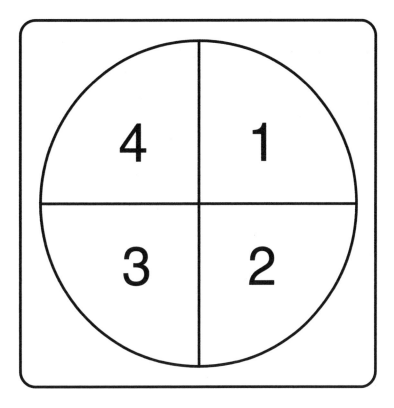

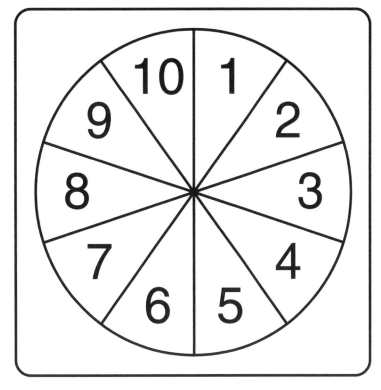

9 to 5 War

This is a card game for two players.

Materials

Both players need two stacks of cards: one stack of 9s and 5s and another stack of cards with other digits.

Getting Ready

- Each partner cuts out the cards on both of the *9 to 5 War Cards* Activity Pages in the *Discovery Assignment Book.* Mix up your cards and place your stack face down in front of you.
- Prepare a second stack of cards with other numbers:

  Each player uses 20 *Digit Cards* (0–9). Mix up your digit cards and place them in a stack in front of you.

  Or, use a deck of playing cards. Remove all the face cards. The ace will be one. Mix up the rest of the cards and divide them equally. Put your share in a stack face down in front of you.

Playing the Game

- Each player turns over two cards, one from the 9s and 5s pile, and one from the other pile.
- Each player should say a number sentence that tells the product of his or her two cards. Whoever has the greater product wins all four cards.
- If there is a tie, then each player turns over two more cards. The player with the greater product of the second pairs wins all eight cards.

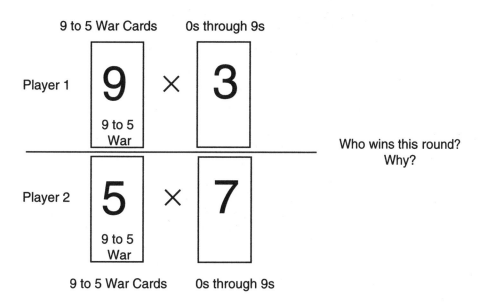

Goal

Play for ten minutes or until the players run out of cards. The player with more cards at the end is the winner.

Variations

1. Whoever has the *smaller* product takes the cards.

2. Play with more than two players.

3. Each player is given only one pile of cards (playing cards with face cards removed or *Digit Cards*). Each player takes the top two cards from his or her pile and multiplies the numbers. The player with the larger product wins all four cards. This game practices all the facts—it does not just focus on the 9s and 5s.

9 to 5 War Cards

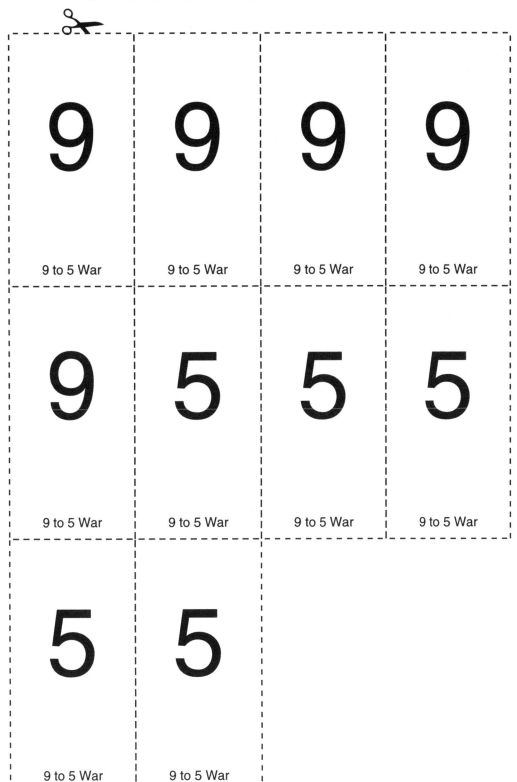

Grade 4 · Facts Resource Guide · Section 6 · Math Facts Games

9 to 5 War Cards

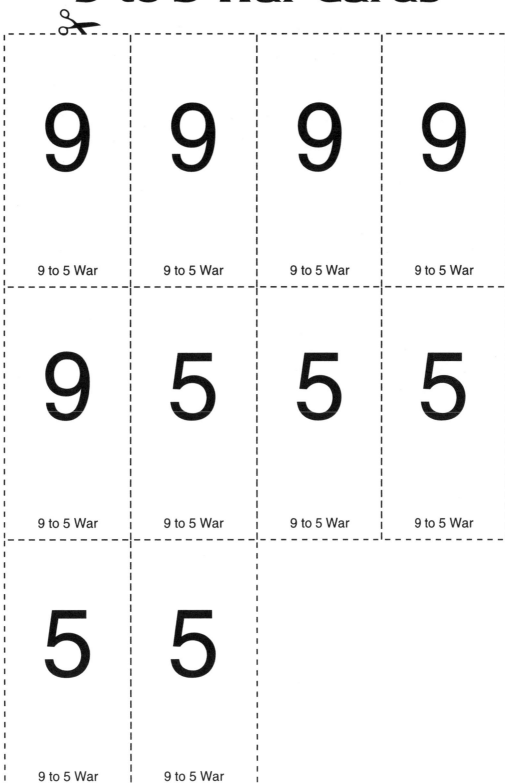

Grade 4 · Facts Resource Guide · Section 6 · Math Facts Games

Name _____   Date _____

4	9
3	8
2	7
1	6
0	5

4	9
3	8
2	7
1	6
0	5

Operation Target

This is a cooperative contest for two or three people. The goal is to use four digits and four operations (+, −, ×, and ÷) to make as many different whole numbers as you can. You need paper, a pencil, and a calculator.

You must use each of the four digits exactly once. You can use operations more than once or not at all. (All division operations must give whole numbers. For example, 9 ÷ 2 = 4.5 is not allowed.)

1. Use 9, 5, 2, and 1 and +, −, ×, and ÷ to make as many whole numbers as you can. For example, 9 + 5 × 2 − 1 = 18. List the numbers you make and show how you made them.

   A. What is the largest whole number you can make?

   B. What is the smallest whole number you can make?

   C. How many whole numbers less than 10 can you make? Write number sentences for each number.

   D. What whole numbers can you make in more than one way? Show at least two number sentences for each.

2. Pick four different digits. Make as many whole numbers as you can using your four new digits and +, −, ×, and ÷. List the numbers you make and show how you made them.

3. Nila used 1, 2, 3, and 4 to make 10. How do you think she did it? Can you think of another way?

4. Luis used 1, 2, 3, and 4 to make 24. How could he have done it?

5. Romesh used 1, 3, 5, and 7 to make 8. How could he have done it?

6. Make up your own problem like Questions 3, 4, and 5.

More Operation Target

Operation Target is a game that can be played many ways. One set of rules from Unit 7 Lesson 1 is on the previous page. Here is another way to play:

- Use the four digits 1, 4, 6, and 8 and four operations (+, −, ×, and ÷).
- You must use each of the four digits exactly once.
- You can use each operation more than once or not at all.
- You can make two-digit numbers by putting two digits together. For example, you can use the numbers 14 or 68.
- No operation should give you a fraction, a decimal, or a negative number.

5. Here is a way to make the number 1:
   4 − 18 ÷ 6 = ? (First, divide: 18 ÷ 6 = 3)
   4 − 3 = 1 (Then, subtract 3 from 4.)

   Find another way to make the number 1 following the new rules.

6. Make at least five numbers using these rules.

7. What is the largest number you can make?

8. What is the smallest number you can make?

Challenge: Make all the numbers from 0 to 9.

Mixed-Up Tables

Homework

Fill in these multiplication tables:

1.

×	2	4	8
2			
4		16	
8			

2.

×	1	3	9
1			
3			
9			

3. What patterns do you see in the table in Question 1?

4. What patterns do you see in the table in Question 2?

5.

×	10	5	0
10			
5			
0			

6.

×	6	5	7
6			
5			
7			

7. What patterns do you see in the table in Question 5?

8. What patterns do you see in the table in Question 6?

9.

×	8	6	4
8			
6			
4			

10.

×	8	6	3
8			
6			
3			

11.

×	2	5	8
9			
4			
7			

12.

×	7	6	4
3			
9			
10			

Fill in these division tables. Divide the large number across the top by the small number on the side.

13. Dividend

÷	24	30	36
2			18
3		10	
6			

Divisor

14. Dividend

÷	16	32	40
2			
4			
8			

Divisor

Triangle Flash Cards: Multiplication and Division

This section includes the multiplication and division *Triangle Flash Cards* for the 2s, 3s, 5s, 9s, 10s, Square Numbers, Last Six Facts, and *Triangle Flash Cards Masters*. See the Math Facts Calendar in Section 4 for when to use each group of *Triangle Flash Cards*.

Using the *Triangle Flash Cards* to Study the Multiplication Facts and Update the *Multiplication Facts I Know* Chart

To use the flash cards to study the multiplication facts, one partner covers the corner containing the highest number with his or her thumb (this number is lightly shaded). This number is the answer to a multiplication problem, the product. The second person multiplies the two uncovered numbers, the factors. Partners should take turns quizzing each other on the multiplication facts.

As a student is quizzed, he or she places each flash card into one of three piles: those facts known and answered quickly, those that can be figured out with a strategy, and those that need to be learned. Once students have sorted all their cards, they circle those facts that they know and can answer quickly on a copy of the *Multiplication Facts I Know* chart that can be found in Section 5 on page 66.

Using the *Triangle Flash Cards* to Study the Division Facts and Update the *Division Facts I Know* Chart

To use the flash cards to study the division facts, one partner covers the number in the square. This number is the answer to the division problem, the quotient. (The number in the circle is the divisor.) The second person solves a division fact using the two uncovered numbers. Partners should take turns quizzing each other on the division facts.

As a student is quizzed, he or she places each flash card into one of three piles: those facts known and answered quickly, those that can be figured out with a strategy, and those that need to be learned. Once students have sorted all their cards, they circle those facts that they know and can answer quickly on a copy of the *Division Facts I Know* chart that can be found in Section 5 on page 133.

Note that each card represents all four facts in a fact family, for example, 6×4, 4×6, $24 \div 6$, and $24 \div 4$. When students are practicing the multiplication facts, remind them of the turn-around facts. If they know $4 \times 6 = 24$, they also know $6 \times 4 = 24$. They should circle both facts on their *Multiplication Facts I Know* charts.

When students are practicing the division facts, they can go through the cards twice, once by covering the number in the circle and once by covering the number in the square. Alternatively, students can go through the cards once and then give the remaining division fact in the fact family. They should circle both facts on their *Division Facts I Know* charts.

Triangle Flash Cards: 2s

- Work with a partner. Each partner cuts out the 9 flash cards.
- Your partner chooses one card at a time and covers one corner.
- To quiz you on a multiplication fact, your partner covers the shaded number. Multiply the two uncovered numbers.
- To quiz you on a division fact, your partner covers the number in the square or the number in the circle. Solve a division fact with the two uncovered numbers.
- Divide the used cards into three piles: those that you know and can answer quickly, those that you can figure out, and those that you need to learn.
- Practice the last two piles again. Then, make a list of the facts you need to practice at home.
- Repeat the directions for your partner.

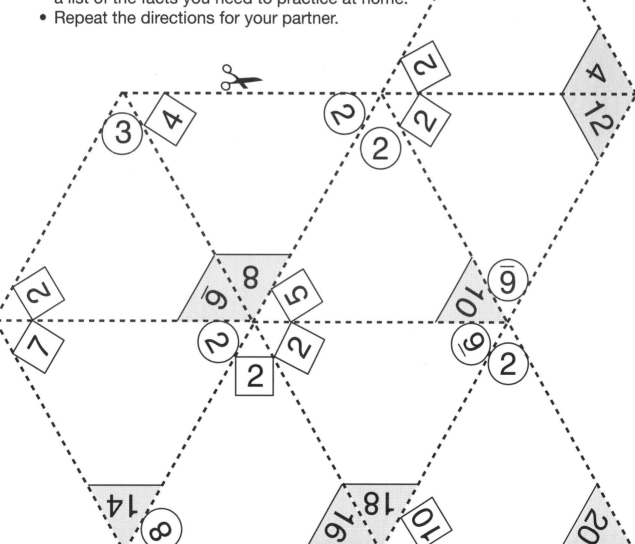

Triangle Flash Cards: 3s

- Work with a partner. Each partner cuts out the 9 flash cards.
- Your partner chooses one card at a time and covers one corner.
- To quiz you on a multiplication fact, your partner covers the shaded number. Multiply the two uncovered numbers.
- To quiz you on a division fact, your partner covers the number in the square or the number in the circle. Solve a division fact with the two uncovered numbers.
- Divide the used cards into three piles: those that you know and can answer quickly, those that you can figure out, and those that you need to learn.
- Practice the last two piles again. Then, make a list of the facts you need to practice at home.
- Repeat the directions for your partner.

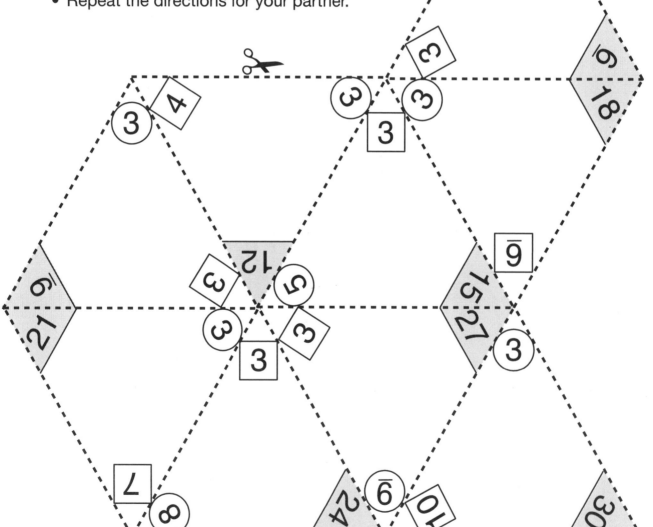

Triangle Flash Cards: 5s

- Work with a partner. Each partner cuts out the 9 flash cards.
- Your partner chooses one card at a time and covers one corner.
- To quiz you on a multiplication fact, your partner covers the shaded number. Multiply the two uncovered numbers.
- To quiz you on a division fact, your partner covers the number in the square or the number in the circle. Solve a division fact with the two uncovered numbers.
- Divide the used cards into three piles: those that you know and can answer quickly, those that you can figure out, and those that you need to learn.
- Practice the last two piles again. Then, make a list of the facts you need to practice at home.
- Repeat the directions for your partner.

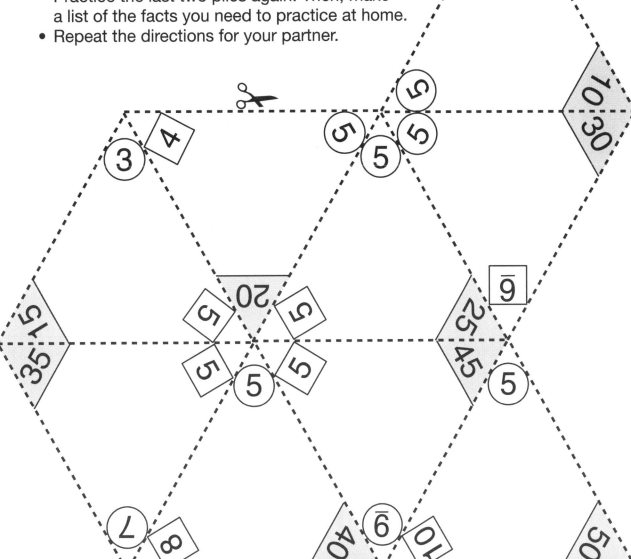

Triangle Flash Cards: 9s

- Work with a partner. Each partner cuts out the 9 flash cards.
- Your partner chooses one card at a time and covers one corner.
- To quiz you on a multiplication fact, your partner covers the shaded number. Multiply the two uncovered numbers.
- To quiz you on a division fact, your partner covers the number in the square or the number in the circle. Solve a division fact with the two uncovered numbers.
- Divide the used cards into three piles: those that you know and can answer quickly, those that you can figure out, and those that you need to learn.
- Practice the last two piles again. Then, make a list of the facts you need to practice at home.
- Repeat the directions for your partner.

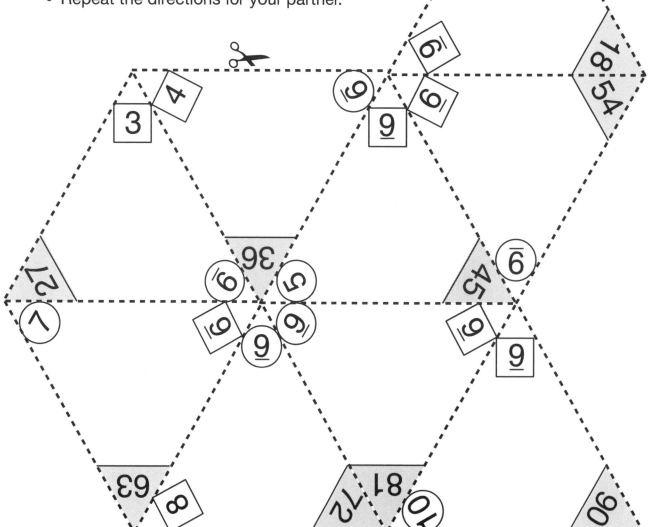

Triangle Flash Cards: 10s

- Work with a partner. Each partner cuts out the 9 flash cards.
- Your partner chooses one card at a time and covers one corner.
- To quiz you on a multiplication fact, your partner covers the shaded number. Multiply the two uncovered numbers.
- To quiz you on a division fact, your partner covers the number in the square or the number in the circle. Solve a division fact with the two uncovered numbers.
- Divide the used cards into three piles: those that you know and can answer quickly, those that you can figure out, and those that you need to learn.
- Practice the last two piles again. Then, make a list of the facts you need to practice at home.
- Repeat the directions for your partner.

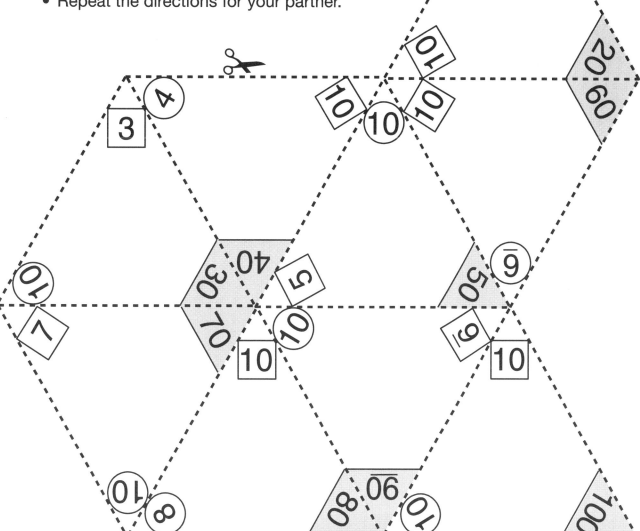

Triangle Flash Cards: Square Numbers

- Work with a partner. Each partner cuts out the 9 flash cards.
- Your partner chooses one card at a time and covers one corner.
- To quiz you on a multiplication fact, your partner covers the shaded number. Multiply the two uncovered numbers.
- To quiz you on a division fact, your partner covers one of the smaller numbers on each card. Solve a division fact with the two uncovered numbers.
- Divide the used cards into three piles: those that you know and can answer quickly, those that you can figure out, and those that you need to learn.
- Practice the last two piles again. Then, make a list of the facts you need to practice at home.
- Repeat the directions for your partner.

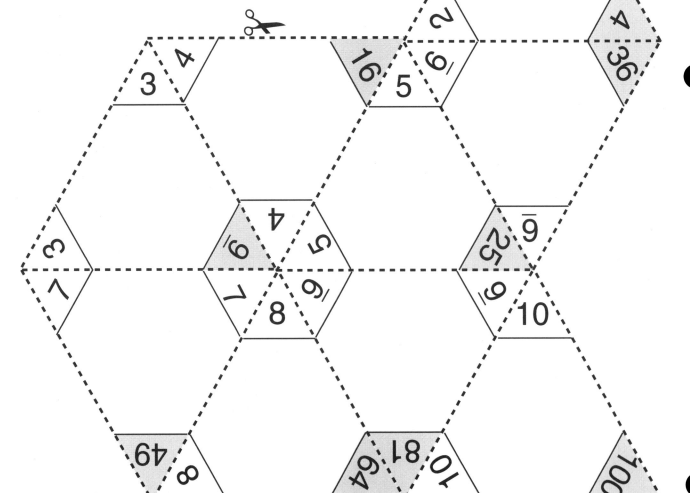

Name _____   Date _____

Triangle Flash Cards: Last Six Facts

- Work with a partner. Each partner cuts out the 6 flash cards.
- Your partner chooses one card at a time and covers one corner.
- To quiz you on a multiplication fact, your partner covers the shaded number. Multiply the two uncovered numbers.
- To quiz you on a division fact, your partner covers the number in the square or the number in the circle. Solve a division fact with the two uncovered numbers.
- Divide the used cards into three piles: those that you know and can answer quickly, those that you can figure out, and those that you need to learn.
- Practice the last two piles again. Then, make a list of the facts you need to practice at home.
- Repeat the directions for your partner.

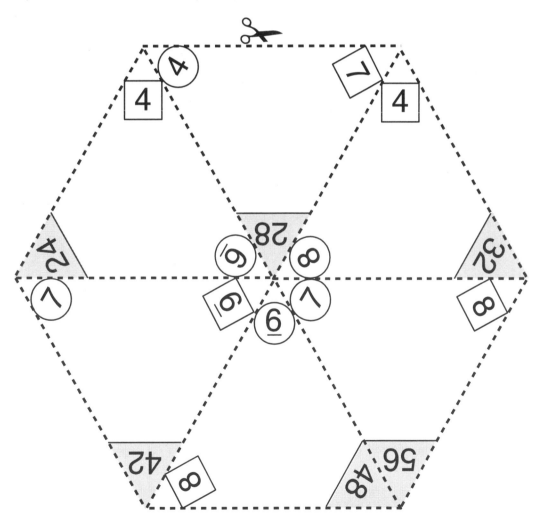

Triangle Flash Card Master

- Make a flash card for each fact that is not circled on your *Multiplication* and *Division Facts I Know* charts. Write the product in the shaded corner of each triangle. Then, cut out the flash cards.
- Your partner chooses one card at a time and covers one corner.
- To quiz you on a multiplication fact, your partner covers the shaded number. Multiply the two uncovered numbers.
- To quiz you on a division fact, your partner covers the number in the square or the number in the circle. Solve a division fact with the two uncovered numbers.
- Practice the last two piles again. Then, make a list of the facts you need to practice at home.
- Repeat the directions for your partner.

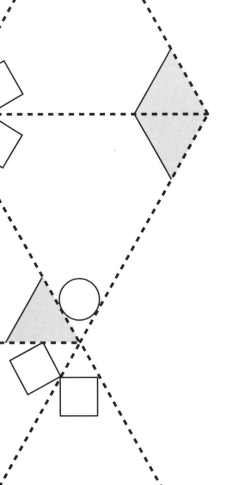

Triangle Flash Card Master

- Make a flash card for each fact that is not circled on your *Multiplication* and *Division Facts I Know* charts. Write the product in the shaded corner of each triangle. Then, cut out the flash cards.
- Your partner chooses one card at a time and covers one corner.
- To quiz you on a multiplication fact, your partner covers the shaded number. Multiply the two uncovered numbers.
- To quiz you on a division fact, your partner covers the number in the square or the number in the circle. Solve a division fact with the two uncovered numbers.
- Practice the last two piles again. Then, make a list of the facts you need to practice at home.
- Repeat the directions for your partner.

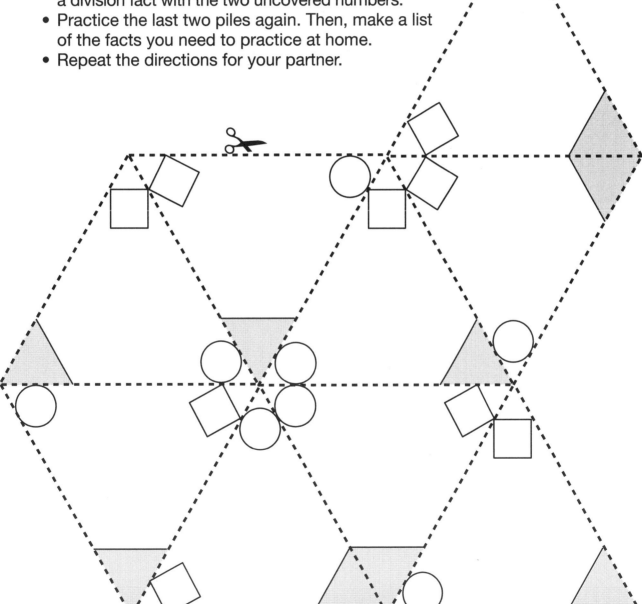

Addition and Subtraction Math Facts Review

The Addition and Subtraction Math Facts Review contains games and activities that can be used by those students who need extra practice with the addition and subtraction facts. Some of the games and activities are from previous grades of the *Math Trailblazers* curriculum.

Items 1K and 1M in the Daily Practice and Problems (DPP) for Unit 1 provide addition facts inventory tests. Items 2M, 2O, 2Q and 2S in Unit 2 provide subtraction facts inventory tests. (These items can be found in Section 5.) Use these tests to see which of your students need more work with the addition and subtraction facts. Those who can find answers quickly and efficiently will continue to practice the addition and subtraction facts throughout the year as they engage in labs, activities, and games, and as they solve problems in the DPP and Home Practice. However, for those students who need extra practice, we have developed games, activities, and flash cards, which can be found in this section.

Use DPP items 1K, 1M, 2M, 2O, 2Q, and 2S from Units 1 and 2 as diagnostic tests to find out which facts individual students need to practice. The following table suggests which activities from this section you should assign to students who do not do well on specific diagnostic tests.

Diagnostic Test	Games and Flash Cards
Addition Test: Doubles, 2s, 3s	Add 1, 2, 3 Path to Glory Path to Glory: 100 Loses Path to Glory: Challenge Triangle Flash Cards for Groups A, B, C, D, E
Addition Test: More Addition Facts	Add 4, 5, 6 Addition War! Mixed-Up Addition Tables 1 and 2 Line Math 1–5 Triangle Flash Cards for Groups C, D, E, F, G
Subtraction Facts: Count-Ups	Subtract 1, 2, 3: 10 Triangle Flash Cards for Groups A, B, C, D
Subtraction Facts: Count-Backs	Path to Glory: Subtraction Subtract 1, 2, 3: 10 Triangle Flash Cards for Groups A, B, C, D
Subtraction Facts: Using a Ten	Subtraction 9 to 5 Triangle Flash Cards for Groups E, F, G
Subtraction Facts: Doubles and Others	Make N: + and − Make N: Challenge Difference War! Triangle Flash Cards for Groups C, D, E

Students should gradually use the activities, games, and flash cards provided in the Addition and Subtraction Math Facts Review at home with family members. They should concentrate on one small group of facts at a time. Practicing small groups of facts often (for short periods of time) is more effective than practicing many facts less often (for long periods of time). While students practice the addition and subtraction facts at home, in class they should be encouraged to use strategies, calculators, and printed addition and subtraction tables. These tools allow students to continue to develop number sense and work on interesting problems and experiments while they are learning the facts. In this way, students who need extra practice are not prevented from learning more complex mathematics because they do not know all the math facts.

After students have been given the opportunity to use some of the items provided in the Addition and Subtraction Math Facts Review, you can administer the appropriate tests a second time to see students' progress. Alternative forms for each test are located at the end of this section. These tests should be administered over a period of time.

For more information about the distribution of the practice and assessment of the math facts in *Math Trailblazers,* see the TIMS Tutor: *Math Facts* in Section 3 and the Assessment section in the *Teacher Implementation Guide.*

Add 1, 2, 3

This is a game for two players.

Directions

1. **Player 1 (P1) adds 1, 2, or 3 to 0 and completes the number sentence:**
   0 + _____ = _____.

2. **Player 2 (P2) adds 1, 2, or 3 to Player 1's answer and records a number sentence.**

3. **Play continues. The player who reaches 10 exactly, wins. A game is started for you.**

P1: 0 + _2_ = _2_

P2: _2_ + _1_ = _3_

P1: _3_ + _3_ = _6_

P2: _6_ + _____ = _____

P1: _____ + _____ = _____

P2: _____ + _____ = _____

P1: _____ + _____ = _____

P2: _____ + _____ = _____

P1: 0 + _____ = _____

P2: _____ + _____ = _____

P1: _____ + _____ = _____

P2: _____ + _____ = _____

P1: _____ + _____ = _____

P2: _____ + _____ = _____

P1: _____ + _____ = _____

P2: _____ + _____ = _____

P1: 0 + _____ = _____

P2: _____ + _____ = _____

P1: _____ + _____ = _____

P2: _____ + _____ = _____

P1: _____ + _____ = _____

P2: _____ + _____ = _____

P1: _____ + _____ = _____

P2: _____ + _____ = _____

P1: 0 + _____ = _____

P2: _____ + _____ = _____

P1: _____ + _____ = _____

P2: _____ + _____ = _____

P1: _____ + _____ = _____

P2: _____ + _____ = _____

P1: _____ + _____ = _____

P2: _____ + _____ = _____

Path to Glory

This is a game for two players.

Directions

Start at 0. Take turns adding 1, 2, 3, 10, 20, or 30. Write each number you add in a circle. Write the sums in the squares as you go. The player who reaches 100 exactly is the winner.

Here is the beginning of a game: 0 —— (+10) → 10 —— (+20) → 30 →

Play 2 or 3 games. Then, write about what happened. Tell how to win.

Path to Glory: 100 Loses

This game is for two players.

Directions

Start at 0. Take turns adding 1, 2, 3, 10, 20, or 30. Write each number you add in a circle. Write the sums in the squares as you go. The player who reaches 100 or more, loses.

Here is the beginning of a game: 0 — (+1) → 1 — (+30) → 31 →

Play 2 or 3 games. Then, write about what happened. Tell how to win.

Path to Glory: Challenge

Directions

Work with a partner. Start at 0. Take turns adding 1, 2, 3, 10, 20, or 30. Write each number you add in a circle. Write the sums in the squares as you go. Can you reach 100 in exactly 11 steps?

Is there another way to reach 100 in exactly 11 steps? Write about what happened.

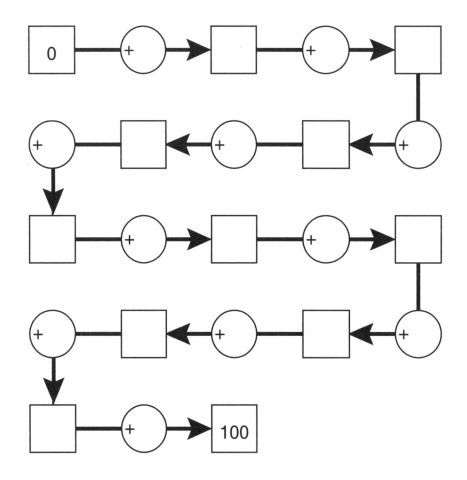

Add 4, 5, 6

This is a game for two players.

Directions

1. **Player 1 (P1) adds 4, 5, or 6 to 0 and completes the number sentence: 0 + _____ = _____.**

2. **Player 2 (P2) adds 4, 5, or 6 to Player 1's answer and records a number sentence.**

3. **Play continues. The player who gets to 30 or more, wins. A game is started for you.**

P1: 0 + _6_ = _6_	P1: 0 + _____ = _____
P2: _6_ + _5_ = _11_	P2: _____ + _____ = _____
P1: _11_ + _4_ = _15_	P1: _____ + _____ = _____
P2: _15_ + _____ = _____	P2: _____ + _____ = _____
P1: _____ + _____ = _____	P1: _____ + _____ = _____
P2: _____ + _____ = _____	P2: _____ + _____ = _____
P1: _____ + _____ = _____	P1: _____ + _____ = _____
P2: _____ + _____ = _____	P2: _____ + _____ = _____

P1: 0 + _____ = _____	P1: 0 + _____ = _____
P2: _____ + _____ = _____	P2: _____ + _____ = _____
P1: _____ + _____ = _____	P1: _____ + _____ = _____
P2: _____ + _____ = _____	P2: _____ + _____ = _____
P1: _____ + _____ = _____	P1: _____ + _____ = _____
P2: _____ + _____ = _____	P2: _____ + _____ = _____
P1: _____ + _____ = _____	P1: _____ + _____ = _____
P2: _____ + _____ = _____	P2: _____ + _____ = _____

Addition War!

This is a card game for two players.

Materials

You need *Digit Cards* with digits 0 to 9 on them.
You can use *Digit Cards* or regular playing cards. (Let the Ace = 1 and the Jack = 0.
Remove the other face cards.)

Directions

1. **Deal out all the cards.**
2. **Each player turns over two cards and says a number sentence that tells the sum of the numbers he or she turned up. Whoever has the larger sum wins all four cards.**
3. **If there is a tie, turn over two more cards. The larger of the second set takes all eight cards.**
4. **Play for ten minutes or until one player runs out of cards. The player with the most cards at the end wins.**

Variations

- Remove 1s, 2s, and 3s for a harder game.
- Whoever has the *smaller* sum takes the cards.
- Play *Subtraction War!* Whoever has the largest difference wins the cards.
- Play with more than two players.

9 8 7 6

Digit Cards   Digit Cards   Digit Cards   Digit Cards

5 4 3 2

Digit Cards   Digit Cards   Digit Cards   Digit Cards

1 0

Digit Cards   Digit Cards

Grade 4 · Facts Resource Guide · Section 8 · Addition and Subtraction Review

Name _____ Date _____

Triangle Flash Cards: Addition and Subtraction

Addition Practice

With a partner, use your *Triangle Flash Cards* to practice the addition or subtraction facts. If you are practicing addition, one partner covers the corner containing the highest number. This number will be the answer to an addition problem. The second person adds the two uncovered numbers.

$9 + 4 = ?$

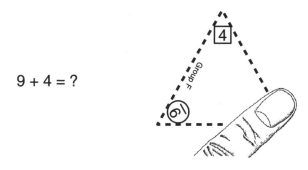

Sorting the Flash Cards

Separate the used cards into three piles: those facts you know and can answer quickly, those that you can figure out with a strategy, and those that you need to learn. Practice the last two piles again and then make a list of the facts you need to practice at home for homework.

Discuss how you can figure out facts you don't recall at once. Share your strategies with your partner.

Subtraction Practice

If you are practicing subtraction, cover the corner with the square. Subtract the uncovered numbers. Then, go through the cards again, this time covering the number in the circle.

$13 - 9 = ?$

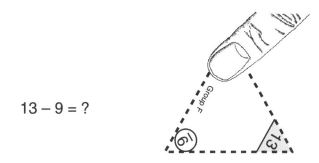

Triangle Flash Cards: Group A

1. Cut out the flash cards.

2. Work with a partner. To practice an addition fact, cover the corner with the highest number. (It is shaded.) Add the two uncovered numbers.

3. Divide the cards into three piles: those facts you know and can answer quickly, those that you can figure out, and those that you need to learn.

4. Practice the last two piles again. Then, make a list of the facts you need to practice.

5. To practice a subtraction fact, cover the corner with the square. Subtract the uncovered numbers. Then go through the cards again, this time covering the number in the circle.

6. Repeat the directions in 3 and 4 above each time you go through the cards.

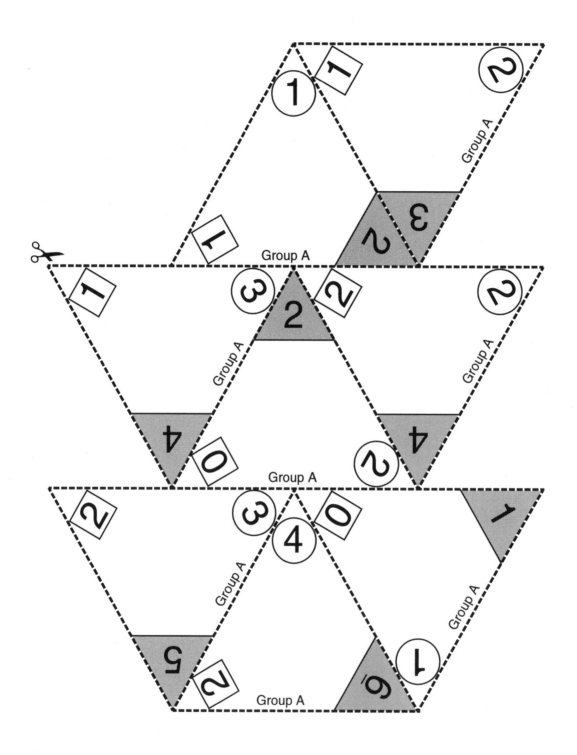

Triangle Flash Cards: Group B

1. Cut out the flash cards.

2. Work with a partner. To practice an addition fact, cover the corner with the highest number. (It is shaded.) Add the two uncovered numbers.

3. Divide the cards into three piles: those facts you know and can answer quickly, those that you can figure out, and those that you need to learn.

4. Practice the last two piles again. Then, make a list of the facts you need to practice.

5. To practice a subtraction fact, cover the corner with the square. Subtract the uncovered numbers. Then go through the cards again, this time covering the number in the circle.

6. Repeat the directions in 3 and 4 above each time you go through the cards.

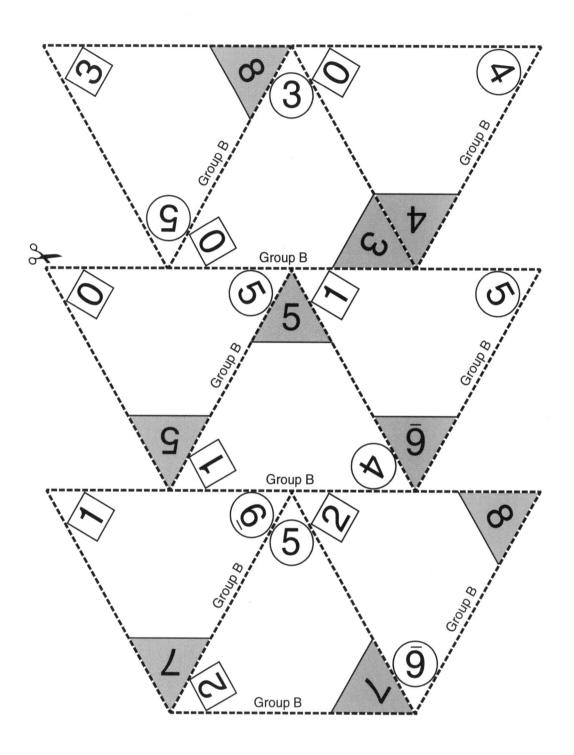

Name _____ Date _____

Triangle Flash Cards: Group C

1. Cut out the flash cards.

2. Work with a partner. To practice an addition fact, cover the corner with the highest number. (It is shaded.) Add the two uncovered numbers.

3. Divide the cards into three piles: those facts you know and can answer quickly, those that you can figure out, and those that you need to learn.

4. Practice the last two piles again. Then, make a list of the facts you need to practice.

5. To practice a subtraction fact, cover the corner with the square. Subtract the uncovered numbers. Then go through the cards again, this time covering the number in the circle.

6. Repeat the directions in 3 and 4 above each time you go through the cards.

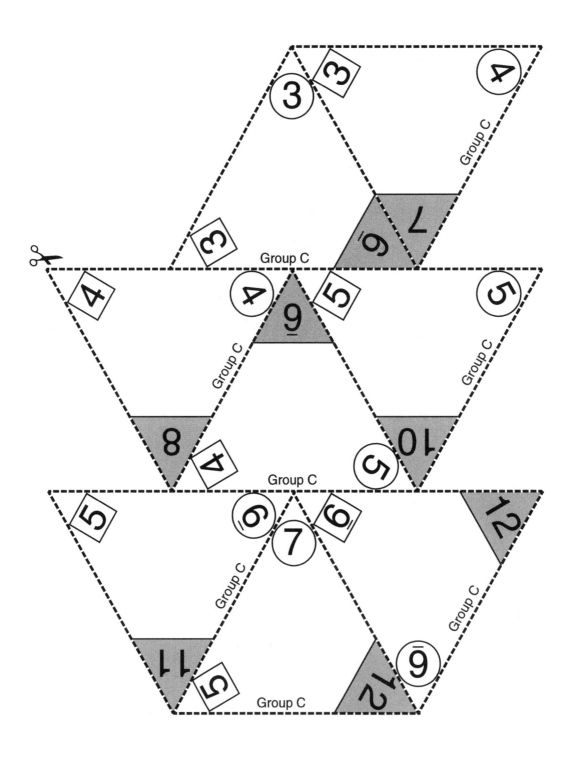

Triangle Flash Cards: Group D

1. Cut out the flash cards.

2. Work with a partner. To practice an addition fact, cover the corner with the highest number. (It is shaded.) Add the two uncovered numbers.

3. Divide the cards into three piles: those facts you know and can answer quickly, those that you can figure out, and those that you need to learn.

4. Practice the last two piles again. Then, make a list of the facts you need to practice.

5. To practice a subtraction fact, cover the corner with the square. Subtract the uncovered numbers. Then go through the cards again, this time covering the number in the circle.

6. Repeat the directions in 3 and 4 above each time you go through the cards.

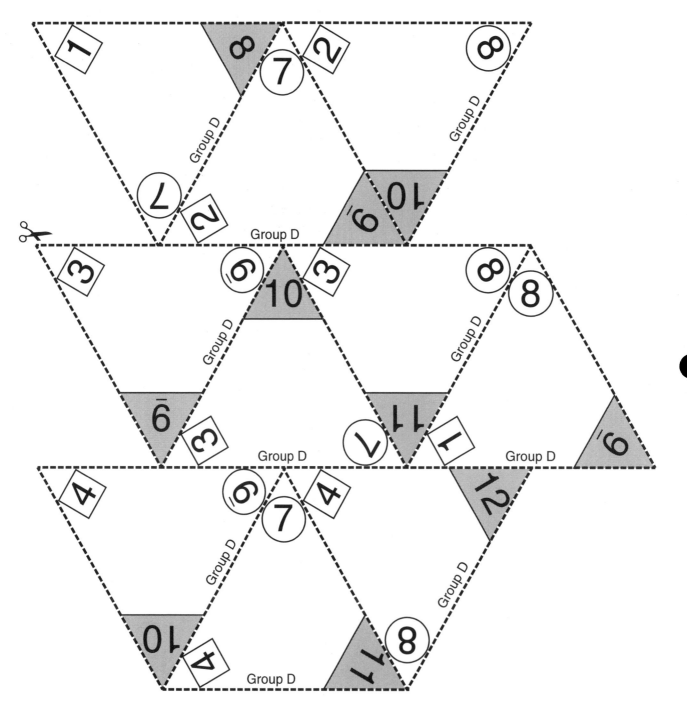

Grade 4 · Facts Resource Guide · Section 8 · Addition and Subtraction Review

Triangle Flash Cards: Group E

1. Cut out the flash cards.

2. Work with a partner. To practice an addition fact, cover the corner with the highest number. (It is shaded.) Add the two uncovered numbers.

3. Divide the cards into three piles: those facts you know and can answer quickly, those that you can figure out, and those that you need to learn.

4. Practice the last two piles again. Then, make a list of the facts you need to practice.

5. To practice a subtraction fact, cover the corner with the square. Subtract the uncovered numbers. Then go through the cards again, this time covering the number in the circle.

6. Repeat the directions in 3 and 4 above each time you go through the cards.

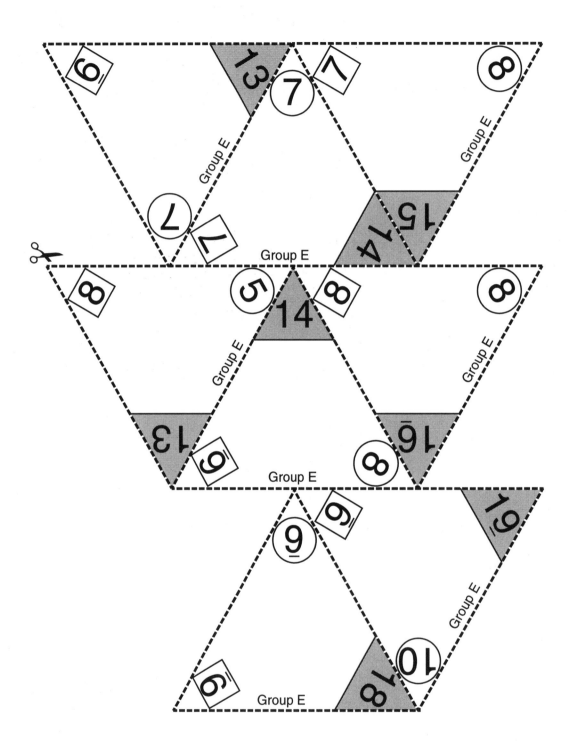

Group E

Group E

Group E

Group E

Group E

Group E

Triangle Flash Cards:
Group F

1. Cut out the flash cards.

2. Work with a partner. To practice an addition fact, cover the corner with the highest number. (It is shaded.) Add the two uncovered numbers.

3. Divide the cards into three piles: those facts you know and can answer quickly, those that you can figure out, and those that you need to learn.

4. Practice the last two piles again. Then, make a list of the facts you need to practice.

5. To practice a subtraction fact, cover the corner with the square. Subtract the uncovered numbers. Then go through the cards again, this time covering the number in the circle.

6. Repeat the directions in 3 and 4 above each time you go through the cards.

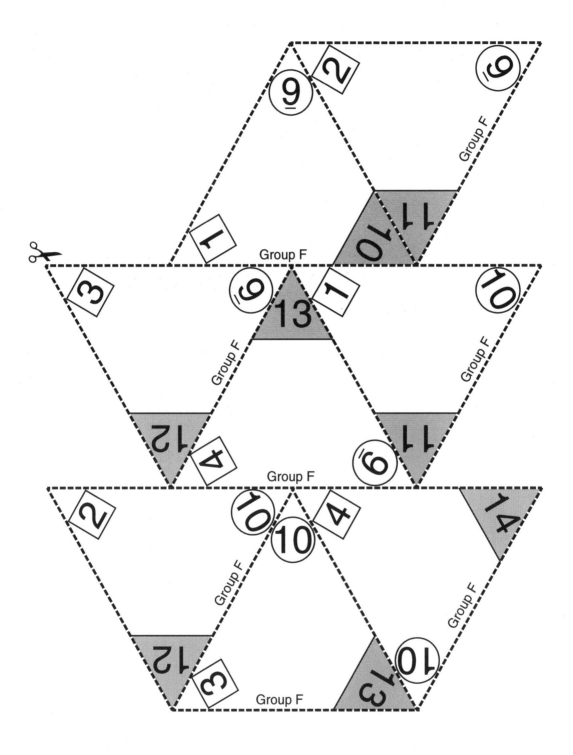

Triangle Flash Cards: Group G

1. Cut out the flash cards.

2. Work with a partner. To practice an addition fact, cover the corner with the highest number. (It is shaded.) Add the two uncovered numbers.

3. Divide the cards into three piles: those facts you know and can answer quickly, those that you can figure out, and those that you need to learn.

4. Practice the last two piles again. Then, make a list of the facts you need to practice.

5. To practice a subtraction fact, cover the corner with the square. Subtract the uncovered numbers. Then go through the cards again, this time covering the number in the circle.

6. Repeat the directions in 3 and 4 above each time you go through the cards.

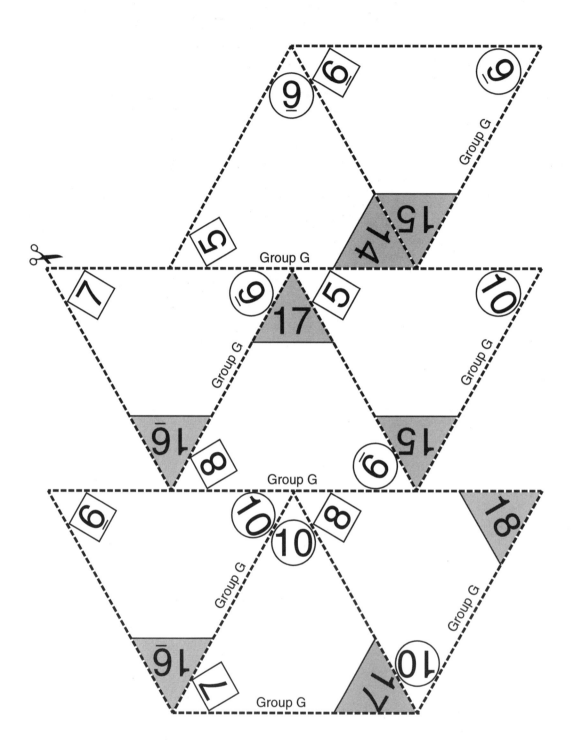

Grade 4 · Facts Resource Guide · Section 8 · Addition and Subtraction Review

Mixed-Up Addition Tables 1

Fill in the missing numbers in these tables.

+	3	6	9	5	7	0
4						
6						
5						
9				14		
8						
7						

+	5	7	8	2	9	6
7						
3						
5						
4						
8						
9						

Mixed-Up Addition Tables 2

Fill in the missing numbers in this table.

+	4	6	2	1	8	7
5						
7						
1						
2		8				
9						
6						

Put your own numbers along the top and left side of this addition table. Ask a friend to complete the table. Check your friend's work.

+						

Line Math 1

Put 1, 2, 3, 4, and 5 in the boxes so that the sum on each line is 9.
Cut out the digits in the dotted boxes to help.

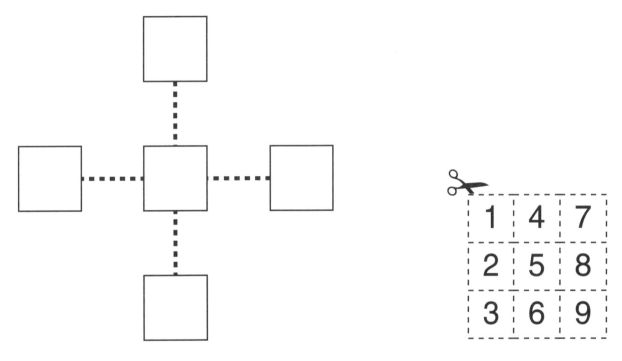

1	4	7
2	5	8
3	6	9

Put 5, 6, 7, 8, and 9 in the boxes so that the sum on each line is 21.

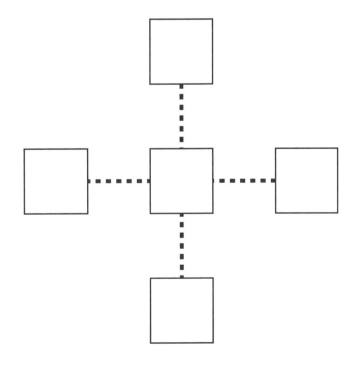

Line Math 2

Put 1, 2, 3, 4, 5, 6, and 7 in the boxes so that the sum on each line is 12. Cut out the digits in the dotted boxes to help.

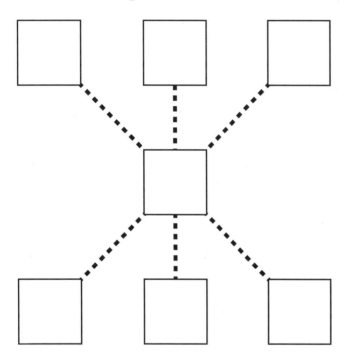

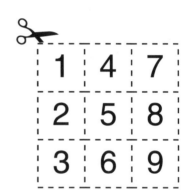

Put 1, 2, 3, 4, 5, and 6 in the boxes so that the sum on each line is 12.

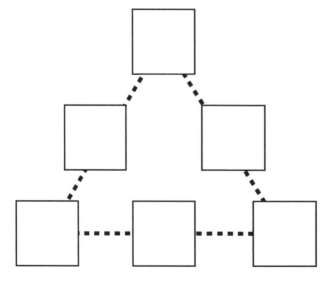

Line Math 3

**Put 1, 2, 3, 4, 5, and 6 in the boxes so that the sum on each line is 9.
Cut out the digits in the dotted boxes to help.**

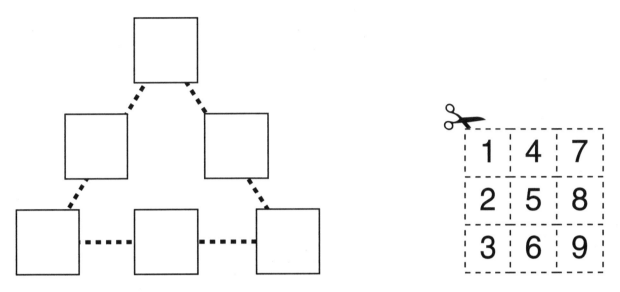

1	4	7
2	5	8
3	6	9

Put 4, 5, 6, 7, 8, and 9 in the boxes so that the sum on each line is 18.

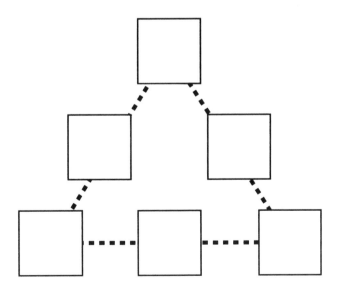

Line Math 4

Put 1, 2, 3, 4, 5, 6, 7, 8, and 9 in the boxes so that the sum on each line is 15. Cut out the digits in the dotted boxes to help.

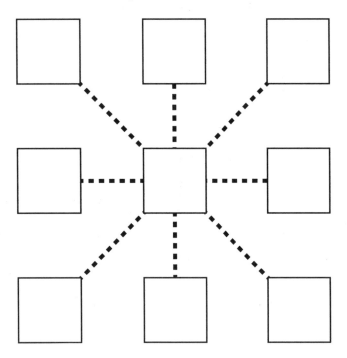

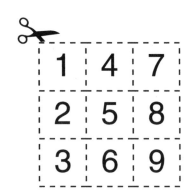

Put 1, 2, 3, 4, 5, 6, 7, 8, and 9 in the boxes so that the sum on each line is 17.

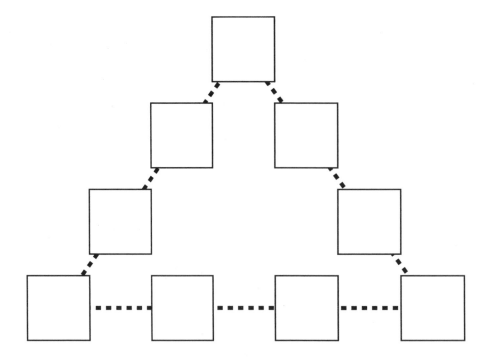

Line Math 5

Put 1, 2, 3, 4, 5, 6, and 7 in the boxes so that the sum on each line is 12. Cut out the digits in the dotted boxes to help.

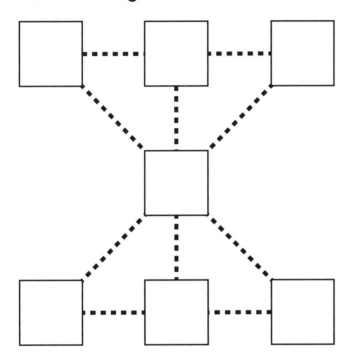

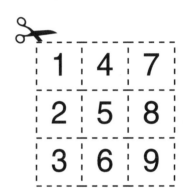

Put 1, 2, 3, 4, 5, 6, 7, 8, and 9 in the boxes so that the sum on each line is 23.

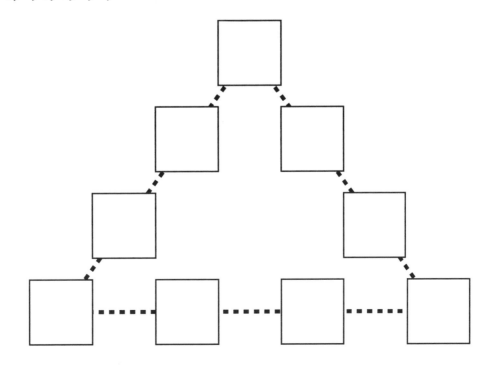

Subtract 1, 2, 3:10

This is a game for two players.

Directions

1. **Player 1 (P1) subtracts 1, 2, or 3 from 10 and completes a number sentence.**

2. **Player 2 (P2) subtracts 1, 2, or 3 from Player 1's answer and records a sentence.**

3. **Play continues. The player who reaches 0 exactly, wins. A game is started for you.**

P1: 10 – _2_ = _8_ P2: _8_ – _1_ = _7_ P1: _7_ – _3_ = _4_ P2: _4_ – ___ = ___ P1: ___ – ___ = ___ P2: ___ – ___ = ___ P1: ___ – ___ = ___ P2: ___ – ___ = ___	P1: 10 – ___ = ___ P2: ___ – ___ = ___ P1: ___ – ___ = ___ P2: ___ – ___ = ___ P1: ___ – ___ = ___ P2: ___ – ___ = ___ P1: ___ – ___ = ___ P2: ___ – ___ = ___
P1: 10 – ___ = ___ P2: ___ – ___ = ___ P1: ___ – ___ = ___ P2: ___ – ___ = ___ P1: ___ – ___ = ___ P2: ___ – ___ = ___ P1: ___ – ___ = ___ P2: ___ – ___ = ___	P1: 10 – ___ = ___ P2: ___ – ___ = ___ P1: ___ – ___ = ___ P2: ___ – ___ = ___ P1: ___ – ___ = ___ P2: ___ – ___ = ___ P1: ___ – ___ = ___ P2: ___ – ___ = ___

Subtraction 9 to 5

This is a game for two players.

Directions

1. Player 1 (P1) subtracts 9, 8, 7, 6, or 5 from 40 and completes a number sentence.

2. Player 2 (P2) subtracts 9, 8, 7, 6, or 5 from Player 1's answer and records a sentence.

3. Play continues. The player who gets to 4 or less first, wins. A game is started for you.

P1: 40 – _9_ = _31_ P2: _31_ – _8_ = _23_ P1: _23_ – _6_ = _17_ P2: _17_ – ___ = ___ P1: ___ – ___ = ___ P2: ___ – ___ = ___ P1: ___ – ___ = ___ P2: ___ – ___ = ___	P1: 40 – ___ = ___ P2: ___ – ___ = ___ P1: ___ – ___ = ___ P2: ___ – ___ = ___ P1: ___ – ___ = ___ P2: ___ – ___ = ___ P1: ___ – ___ = ___ P2: ___ – ___ = ___
P1: 40 – ___ = ___ P2: ___ – ___ = ___ P1: ___ – ___ = ___ P2: ___ – ___ = ___ P1: ___ – ___ = ___ P2: ___ – ___ = ___ P1: ___ – ___ = ___ P2: ___ – ___ = ___	P1: 40 – ___ = ___ P2: ___ – ___ = ___ P1: ___ – ___ = ___ P2: ___ – ___ = ___ P1: ___ – ___ = ___ P2: ___ – ___ = ___ P1: ___ – ___ = ___ P2: ___ – ___ = ___

Path to Glory: Subtraction

This is a game for two players.

Directions

Start at 100. Take turns subtracting 1, 2, 3, 10, 20, or 30. Write each number you subtract in a circle. Write what remains in the squares as you go. The player who reaches 0 exactly, wins.

Here is the beginning of a game: 100 — (−30) → 70 — (−20) → 50 →

Play 2 or 3 games. Then, write about what happened. Tell how to win.

Name _____ Date _____

Make N: + and –

This is an activity for two players.

Materials

You need *Digit Cards* (0, 1, 2, 3, 4, 5, 6, 7, 8, and 9).
You also need *Make N Cards* with the addition sign (+), the subtraction or minus sign (–), the equal sign (=), and the letter *N*.

Directions

1. Work with your partner. Use the cards to make a number sentence for each: $N = 1$, $N = 2$, $N = 3$, . . .

2. Use each digit only once in a number sentence. You can use + and – as often as you like.
   For example, for $N = 10$, one number sentence is $5 + 3 + 2 = N$.
   Another number sentence for $N = 10$ is $N = 6 + 3 + 2 - 1$.

3. Write down your number sentence in the space below. Work in order, starting with $N = 1$.

4. Both partners should check that the number sentence is correct.

Use another sheet of paper if you need more room. An example for $N = 1$ is shown. Find another sentence for $N = 1$.

$N = 1$ _____ $9 - 5 - 3 = N$ _____ $N = 7$ _____

$N = 2$ _____ $N = 8$ _____

$N = 3$ _____ $N = 9$ _____

$N = 4$ _____ $N = 10$ _____

$N = 5$ _____ $N = 11$ _____

$N = 6$ _____ $N = 12$ _____

Name _____   Date _____

✂ -

9   8   7   6

Digit Cards   Digit Cards   Digit Cards   Digit Cards

5   4   3   2

Digit Cards   Digit Cards   Digit Cards   Digit Cards

1   0

Digit Cards   Digit Cards

Grade 4 · Facts Resource Guide · Section 8 · Addition and Subtraction Review

Name _____ Date _____

✂ ---

+	−	+	−
Make N	Make N	Make N	Make N
N	N	=	=
Make N	Make N	Make N	Make N
+	−	+	−
Make N	Make N	Make N	Make N

Make N: Challenge

This is an activity for two partners.

Materials

You need *Digit Cards* (0, 1, 2, 3, 4, 5, 6, 7, 8, and 9).
You also need *Make N Cards* with the addition sign (+), the subtraction or minus sign (−), the equal sign (=), and cards with *N* on them.

Directions

Make N: Challenge is almost the same as *Make N: + and −*. But the goal of this game is to use as many digits as possible.

1. Work with your partner. Use the cards to make a number sentence for each: *N* = 1, *N* = 2, *N* = 3, . . .

2. Use each digit only once in a number sentence. Try to use as many digits as you can. Use + and − as often as you like.
   For example, for *N* = 23, one number sentence is 9 + 8 + 6 = *N*.
   But the sentence 9 + 8 + 7 − 6 + 5 = *N* uses more digits, so in this game it's better.

3. Write down your number sentence in the space below. Work in order, starting with *N* = 1.

4. Both partners should check that the number sentence is correct.

Use another sheet of paper if you need more room.

N = 1 _____	*N* = 7 _____
N = 2 _____	*N* = 8 _____
N = 3 _____	*N* = 9 _____
N = 4 _____	*N* = 10 _____
N = 5 _____	*N* = 11 _____
N = 6 _____	*N* = 12 _____

Difference War!

This is a card game for two players.

Materials

You need *Difference War Cards* (these have the numbers 7, 8, 9, and 10 on them and a few cards with 5, 6, 11, and 12). You can also make a few cards with your own numbers.

Directions

1. **Deal out all the cards.**

2. **Each player turns over two cards.**

3. **Each player says or writes a number sentence that tells the difference between the numbers you turn up. Whoever has the greater difference wins all four cards.**

4. **If there is a tie, turn over two more cards. The greater difference between the second pair takes all eight cards.**

5. **The player with the most cards at the end wins.**

Variations

- Play with all the digits.
- Whoever has the smaller difference takes the cards.
- Play *Addition War!* Whoever has the largest sum wins the cards.

Name _____ Date _____

✂ -

7	**8**	**9**	**10**
Difference War!	Difference War!	Difference War!	Difference War!
7	**8**	**9**	**10**
Difference War!	Difference War!	Difference War!	Difference War!
7	**8**	**9**	**10**
Difference War!	Difference War!	Difference War!	Difference War!

Grade 4 · Facts Resource Guide · Section 8 · Addition and Subtraction Review

Name _____   Date _____

✂

5	6	11	12
Difference War!	Difference War!	Difference War!	Difference War!

5	6	11	12
Difference War!	Difference War!	Difference War!	Difference War!

Difference War!	Difference War!	Difference War!	Difference War!

More Doubles, 2s, 3s

5 + 3 = _____   8 + 8 = _____

7 + 7 = _____   2 + 4 = _____

6 + 3 = _____   6 + 6 = _____

3 + 8 = _____   3 + 3 = _____

9 + 9 = _____   3 + 4 = _____

6 + 2 = _____   7 + 3 = _____

2 + 7 = _____   2 + 8 = _____

5 + 5 = _____   4 + 4 = _____

Even More Addition Facts

7 + 9 = _____   6 + 8 = _____

4 + 7 = _____   9 + 5 = _____

7 + 6 = _____   8 + 9 = _____

5 + 7 = _____   4 + 6 = _____

7 + 8 = _____   9 + 4 = _____

4 + 5 = _____   8 + 5 = _____

9 + 6 = _____   4 + 8 = _____

6 + 5 = _____   9 + 3 = _____

10 + 4 = _____   9 + 10 = _____

More Subtraction Facts: Count-Ups

8 − 6 = _____

11 − 8 = _____

9 − 6 = _____

9 − 7 = _____

10 − 8 = _____

6 − 4 = _____

9 − 5 = _____

7 − 4 = _____

10 − 7 = _____

5 − 3 = _____

8 − 7 = _____

7 − 5 = _____

7 − 6 = _____

6 − 3 = _____

6 − 5 = _____

8 − 5 = _____

Name _____ Date _____

More Subtraction Facts: Count-Backs

8 – 2 = _____

9 – 1 = _____

4 – 3 = _____

10 – 2 = _____

9 – 3 = _____

5 – 0 = _____

5 – 2 = _____

10 – 3 = _____

9 – 2 = _____

7 – 2 = _____

11 – 2 = _____

8 – 1 = _____

8 – 3 = _____

11 – 3 = _____

4 – 2 = _____

6 – 2 = _____

More Subtraction Facts: Using a Ten

17 − 9 = _____   13 − 8 = _____

16 − 7 = _____   13 − 9 = _____

16 − 6 = _____   15 − 7 = _____

17 − 8 = _____   16 − 9 = _____

15 − 10 = _____   12 − 2 = _____

18 − 8 = _____   17 − 10 = _____

15 − 9 = _____   14 − 9 = _____

14 − 4 = _____   13 − 7 = _____

11 − 9 = _____   14 − 8 = _____

More Subtraction Facts: Doubles and Others

11 − 5 = _____   14 − 7 = _____

10 − 4 = _____   12 − 5 = _____

16 − 8 = _____   10 − 5 = _____

15 − 8 = _____   12 − 6 = _____

18 − 9 = _____   11 − 6 = _____

13 − 6 = _____   13 − 5 = _____

12 − 4 = _____   9 − 4 = _____

15 − 6 = _____   11 − 4 = _____